MUFFINS
GALORE

MUFFINS
GALORE

WITHDRAWN

CATHERINE ATKINSON

Published by MQ Publications Limited

12 The Ivories, 6–8 Northampton Street

London N1 2HY

Tel: 44 (0)20 7359 2244

Fax: 44 (0)20 7359 1616

email: mail@mqpublications.com

North American office

49 West 24th Street

New York, NY 10010

Email: information@mqpublicationsus.com

Website: www.mqpublications.com

Copyright © MQ Publications Limited 2006

PHOTOGRAPHY: Marie Louise Avery

HOME ECONOMIST: Kim Morphew

STYLIST: Rachel Jukes

RECIPE CREDITS: see page 192

ISBN 10: 1-84601-123-X

ISBN 13: 78-1-84601-123-8

1 3 5 7 9 0 8 6 4 2

CONTENTS

INTRODUCTION

When it comes to a quick-and-easy treat, nothing beats freshly baked, mouthwatering muffins. This fabulous recipe collection has more than 100 flavor combinations for every occasion, from sweet and sticky muffins to savory and healthy, wholesome varieties.

★ AN AMERICAN INVENTION ★

The name "muffin" is given to two very different types of baked goods: one, the yeast-leavened English muffin, was known as far back as the 11th century. This thick, flat bun is served split and toasted and lavishly buttered at the American breakfast table and is also a traditional English tea-time treat, although the name comes from the French "moufflet," meaning a soft bread. The other, an American invention, began as a yeast bread but gradually evolved to be a "quick bread" (that is, a dough risen chemically using a leavening agent rather than yeast). Quite distinguishable from its English counterpart, it's this type of muffin that features in this book.

★ EARLY MUFFINS ★

The true tale of the American muffin remains a bit of a mystery, as recipes were kept a secret within families and small communities. They were, however, featured in cookery books at the end of the 18th century when "pearl ash" (potassium carbonate) was discovered in America. This was a refined form of potash, which produced carbon dioxide when mixed with an acid and a liquid, or with an acidic liquid such as soured milk. Housewives no longer needed to wait for the action of yeast to leaven their baked goods. Made quickly and simply, muffins were first served as a hot breakfast food. Gradually different kinds of grains were used, such as corn, wheat, and oatmeal, and a small range of flavors were created with berries, apples, raisins, and nuts. Early versions were much less sweet than contemporary ones and remained very bread-like with little fat. This was mainly because pearl ash produced a soapy taste when combined with butter or lard, so only very small quantities of these could be added to the mixture if the muffin was to remain edible!

This changed when a few decades later sodium bicarbonate—now known as baking soda—was used to make muffins. It worked in exactly the same way as pearl ash in the presence of an acid and a liquid, but with no soapy aftertaste. A few years later, when baking powder was created, muffins could be made without an acid; flavors such as chocolate and coffee began to be used in muffins. At first muffins were baked in "gem irons"—ridged lozenge-shaped pans. With the invention of paper muffin cups, these difficult-to-clean pans quickly lost popularity and circular-shaped muffins became the norm. In the 1950s, packaged muffin mixes became available in the supermarkets, and the popularity and variety of muffins grew at a rapid rate. A decade later, they were in such demand that chains of coffee shop-style muffin eateries started appearing both in America and around the world.

★ MUFFIN-MAKING TODAY ★

In more recent years, there has been a resurgence in home baking as many consumers have turned away from commercially produced products packed with artificial additives. No store-bought muffin can match one that is made from fresh ingredients and the pleasure that home baking provides. For today's busy cook, whether a novice or experienced, muffins, which can be mixed and cooked in minutes, are the perfect baked good. Nowadays, the range of ingredients is vast and so are the possible combinations. The only limitation in muffin-making is your own imagination.

EQUIPMENT

Unlike cakes and cookies, very few specialist items are needed for muffins; they can be made with nothing more sophisticated than a set of measuring cups and spoons, a mixing bowl and spoon, and a muffin pan or a few paper muffin cups on a baking tray. However, using the right equipment will simplify muffin-making and ensure success every time.

★ MEASURING UTENSILS ★

Accurate measuring cups are essential when making muffins. You also need a set of measuring spoons, particularly when adding baking powder and baking soda. For measuring liquid, use a clearly calibrated measuring cup, in glass, plastic, or stainless steel.

★ BOWLS ★

Whether you choose a glass, ceramic, or stainless-steel bowl, make sure that it is large enough to contain both the dry and wet ingredients and that it has enough room for easy mixing. A deep bowl is preferable to a wide, shallow one. In addition, small heat-proof bowls are useful for melting butter or chocolate and for beating eggs.

★ SIFTER ★

In most muffin recipes, it is unnecessary to sift the dry ingredients. A sifter is useful, however, for making frostings for topping muffins and for dusting powdered sugar or cocoa powder over baked muffins. You can also buy a sugar or cocoa shaker or a very fine mesh for this purpose.

★ TIMER ★

This is essential because a few extra minutes in the oven can result in overcooked, dry muffins. Many modern ovens are fitted with a timer; if not, a digital timer or one with a rotating dial and a loud ring is a good investment.

★ WIRE RACK ★

After baking, muffins should be transferred to a wire rack, even if you are planning to serve them warm. The rack will allow air to circulate under the muffins and prevent them from getting soggy.

★ SPATULA ★

A flexible plastic or rubber spatula can be used to scrape the last little bit of muffin mixture from the bowl. It can also be used to fold the dry and wet ingredients together.

★ MUFFINS PANS ★

These vary greatly in quality and if you're an ethusiastic muffin-maker, it's worth buying a heavyweight muffin pan that will absorb and hold heat, helping your muffins rise higher and have a better color. A non-stick pan is preferable as some types of muffins are better made directly in the pan rather than in paper cups. Muffin pans come in a variety of sizes, but the standard version has 12 cups, each about 3 inches in diameter and $1\frac{1}{4}$ inches deep. Mini muffin tins are also popular; again they have 12 holes, but these are a dainty $1\frac{1}{2}$ inches in diameter and $\frac{3}{4}$ inch deep. The new non-stick silicone muffin molds are very handy as they can be used at high temperatures without any additional preparation. They are extremely easy to clean and in some types the material bends, allowing the muffins to pop out easily. You do, however, need to place a baking sheet under the flexible ones to provide some stability.

★ PAPER MUFFIN CUPS ★

You can lightly grease muffin pans, but for ease, paper muffin cups make a great alternative. Not only do they save time and washing up, but they also help keep muffins fresh and make packing muffins for cold lunches and picnics a cinch. Plain pleated white paper cups are the most economical, but there is also a huge range of fancy designs for every occasion available at supermarkets and specialty shops.

★ PIPING BAGS AND TIPS ★

These are useful for piping whipped cream, frostings, icing and melted chocolate when decorating cooled muffins. Most piping bags are now made of nylon; the best are glued and double stitched along the seams to prevent splitting or leakage. You can also buy disposable plastic piping bags, or make your own from greaseproof paper or baking parchment.

★ PASTRY BRUSHES ★

While it's easy to drizzle sticky glazes such as honey, maple syrup and hot sugar syrups over muffins with a teaspoon, a pastry brush will give an all-over, even finish. Choose a brush with either natural bristles fixed in a wooden handle or one with nylon bristles and a plastic handle. After use, rinse in cold water, then wash in hot soapy water, flick dry and leave to air before using again.

★ AIRTIGHT CONTAINERS ★

Most muffins keep well if stored in an airtight plastic or metal container in a cool place. A large shallow one, which will hold the muffins in a single layer is preferable. As a general guide, muffins will keep for around 3–5 days.

★ PLASTIC FREEZER BAGS ★

All of the muffins in this book can be frozen prior to being iced or decorated, unless otherwise indicated. The easiest way to do this is in re-sealable plastic freezer bags, clearly marked with the date the muffins were made. Muffins can be kept frozen for up to 3 months.

INGREDIENTS

Muffins are made from only a few basics—butter or oil, sugar, flour, eggs, and flavorings—so good-quality ingredients are at the heart of successful muffin-making.

★ FLOUR ★

Muffins are made with either ordinary all-purpose or self-rising flour, as these have low gluten content, resulting in a soft, cake-like texture. Self-rising flour contains leavening agents, but often extra baking powder and/or baking soda is added as well to make the muffins really light. Always check the "use-by" date as leavening agents gradually deteriorate. If you want to substitute all-purpose flour for self-rising in a recipe, you will need to add 1 teaspoon for every $2/3$ cup of flour. Whole-wheat flour is milled from the whole wheat kernel and is coarser in texture, giving a heavier result, so is often combined with all-purpose flour.

★ NON WHEAT FLOUR ★

Cornmeal, also known as polenta , has tiny bright yellow grains and is particularly good in savoury muffins. Use medium-ground cornmeal, unless the recipe states otherwise.

Cornflour is a fine white powder made from cornmeal. Used in small quantities in muffins combined with flour, it gives a lighter, smooth texture.

Soy flour is made by grinding soy beans to a powder. It has a distinctive nutty taste and is useful for making gluten-free muffins.

Rice flour, produced by finely grinding white or brown rice, is also useful in gluten-free cooking. It gives muffins a light, slightly crumbly texture.

★ LEAVENING AGENTS ★

Leavening agents react in contact with water and produce carbon dioxide bubbles, so it is essential to bake muffins as soon as they have been mixed. Baking powder is a mixture of alkaline baking soda and an acid such as cream of tartar. Baking soda needs an acid ingredient as well as a liquid in order to work, so is often used in citrus-based muffins and those with buttermilk or yogurt. Store leavening agents in a dry place and use within their "use-by" date as they deteriorate when kept.

★ BUTTER ★

Butter keeps muffins moist and adds a distinct flavor and color. When making muffins with melted butter, cut it into small pieces, so that it melts quickly, and place in a saucepan (or microwave it in a bowl) over low heat to prevent it from burning. Remove it from the heat when it has almost melted and allow the residual heat to finish the job.

For rubbed-in muffin mixtures, remove the butter from the fridge about 10 minutes before using, so that it is still cold but not too hard. For creamed mixtures, let the butter come to room temperature, so that it is soft and easy to beat. If you use butter to grease muffin pans, choose unsalted, as salted butter may make the muffin edges stick. Margarine may be used as an alternative to butter for muffins. It won't produce quite the same flavor as butter, but is usually less expensive.

★ OIL ★

Oil is sometimes used in muffins instead of solid fat. It's especially good in quick-mix muffins because, unlike butter, it doesn't need to be melted and cooled first.

★ SUGAR ★

Sugar is essential in many muffin recipes, including savory ones, to achieve a good texture, but the quality can usually be increased or decreased slightly to suit personal taste. There are many different types of sugar, each with different characteristics.

Superfine sugar is the most frequently used in muffin-making, as it has a fine grain, which combines well with other ingredients. Unrefined superfine sugar is a pale gold color.

Granulated sugar has large granules and is used for crunchy toppings and sometimes in rubbed-in mixtures. You can use regular granulated sugar in any of these recipes (note the change in measurement), or, if you have a spice grinder, you can pulse granulated sugar into a finer texture.

Demerara is a deep golden color with a toffee-like flavor and even larger granules. It's particularly good for sprinkling over the tops of muffins before baking.

Light and dark brown sugar are refined white sugars that have been tossed in syrup or molasses to darken the color and to flavor them. Brown sugar makes moister muffins than superfine sugar, so if you substitute one for the other, add a tiny bit less or more liquid to compensate.

Powdered sugar is ground to a fine powder. It is rarely used in muffin mixtures but makes smooth icings and frostings and may be dusted over the tops of muffins for an easy, professional finish.

Other sweeteners may be used in muffins, including light corn syrup, maple syrup, and honey.

★ EGGS ★

Most of the recipes in this book use medium eggs, unless stated otherwise. Always use eggs at room temperature as cold eggs may curdle and cold egg whites will produce less volume when whisked.

★ FRUIT & NUTS ★

Dried and candied fruit, including apples, apricots, tropical fruits, sour cherries, cranberries and blueberries and small whole or chopped nuts may be added to your favorite muffin mix without altering the consistency of the batter. If you want to add fresh fruit, it is better to use a recipe written for this, as the additional moisture will affect the final result.

zest—use unwaxed fruit if possible—and salt, which helps bring out the flavor in both sweet and savory muffins. If you prefer, you can use a low-sodium substitute.

★ CHOCOLATE ★

Chocolate muffins may be made either with cocoa powder or by stirring melted or chopped chocolate into the batter. Chocolate chips are a quick way to add chocolate flavor and come in milk, white, and semi-sweet varieties. For the very best flavor, use semi-sweet chocolate with at least 70% cocoa solids.

★ SPICES & FLAVORINGS ★

These are a great way to add flavor to muffins, and warm spices, such as cinnamon and ginger, work particularly well in sweet muffins. Vanilla is probably the most frequently added spice and provides a delicate, subtle flavor. Choose pure vanilla extract if you can. Other useful muffin flavorings are grated citrus

SEVEN STEPS TO
successful muffin-making

Muffins are quick and easy to make, but there is some basic know-how that will make them even easier. Follow these seven simple steps and every batch you bake will be perfect.

★ NO.1—PREPARING PANS ★

Spread an even layer of vegetable oil, melted unsalted butter or margarine on the bottom and sides of each cup with a pastry brush or kitchen paper. Do not use too much, however, or the muffins will fry instead of bake. Pleated paper cups provide an easy alternative to greasing the pans.

★ NO.2—MAKING THE MIXTURE ★

Always measure ingredients, particularly flour and liquid, very carefully. There are two ways of making muffins. The most popular is known in culinary terms as "the muffin method." This is the classic way: quick and easy. To get the right consistency, start by thoroughly

combining the dry ingredients in a large mixing bowl and making a well in the middle. Combine the liquid ingredients, then pour them into the well. Use a rubber spatula or spoon to gently combine and moisten the dry ingredients. Stop mixing while the batter is still lumpy; the lumps will disappear when the muffins are baked.

The second is referred to as "the creaming method." This is slightly more time-consuming and produces cake-like muffins. This can also be divided into seven steps:

1. Preheat the oven and prepare the muffin pans.

2. Cream the butter until really light and fluffy.

3. Add the eggs, one at a time, beating well after each addition.

4. Combine the dry ingredients in a separate bowl to evenly distribute the leavening.

5. Gradually add the dry ingredients to the egg mixture, alternating with any liquid and flavorings.

6. Stir the batter until it is just combined; it should still have a few lumps in it.

7. Spoon the batter into the muffin pans or cups, add any topping and bake right away.

★ NO.3—ADDING EXTRA INGREDIENTS ★

Stir ingredients such as dried fruit, nuts, and chocolate chips into the dry ingredients before liquid is added. Moist and soft ingredients such as berries should be added when the batter is half-mixed to avoid crushing them. Gently fold them in, using a down, up and over motion, to ensure that they are distributed evenly through the mixture.

★ NO.4—FILLING THE PANS ★

Once the batter is mixed, the baking agent has been activated, so you need to get the muffins into the oven as soon as possible; the pans should already be greased or lined with paper cups and any toppings should be prepared. Scoop up the batter with a large spoon and push it off the spoon into the prepared pans using another spoon. Fill standard cups about two-thirds full and mini muffin tins just a little higher. If you want really large, mushroom-shaped muffins, fill the cups almost to the rim, but grease the entire top of the muffin pan first to prevent the tops of the muffins from sticking to the area around each cup.

★ NO.5—BAKING ★

It's essential to preheat the oven before you start mixing your muffins. Bake the muffins as soon as you've filled the pans, on the middle oven shelf or just a little higher. Close the oven door as quickly as possible to prevent heat from being lost. Bake the muffins for a minute less than the recommended cooking time and check to see if they are done (if you have a clear glass oven door, you can do this without opening the oven). You can test if they're done by inserting a toothpick or the tip of a knife into the center of one of the muffins. If it comes out clean, the muffins are done. If any batter clings to the toothpick or knife, allow the muffins to bake for another 1–2 minutes. Remove them when they are just ready, as they will continue cooking in the residual heat of the tin.

★ NO.6—REMOVING FROM THE PAN ★

As soon as you remove the muffins from the oven, place the pan on a wire cooling rack, then leave the muffins to stand for 4–5 minutes or for the time recommended in the recipe (moist muffins such as chocolate ones may need longer to firm up). Don't

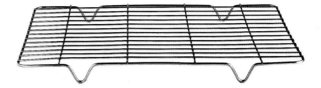

leave muffins in the tin for longer than 10 minutes, or they may be difficult to remove. Carefully loosen muffins from the tin by running a small spatula around the side, then lift out and place on the wire rack to prevent the bottoms from getting soggy.

★ NO.7—STORING ★

Many muffins are best served and eaten warm; others are equally good when cold. Because homemade muffins do not contain preservatives, they should be stored in an airtight container as soon as they are cool. They are best eaten fresh on the day you make them, but most will keep well for 3–4 days. Keep those covered with a butter-based icing, or that contain ingredients such as fresh fruit, cheese or ham, in the fridge. Muffins can also be frozen for up to 3 months and will take about 30 minutes to thaw at room temperature or just a few seconds in the microwave.

★ TOPPING IDEAS ★

A tasty topping adds the final flourish to muffins and can turn an ordinary standby into a really special treat. It can range from a simple sprinkling of sugar or nuts, to brushing with a shiny glaze or a swirl of colorful frosting. Where quantities of ingredients are given, there is sufficient to top 10–12 standard-size muffins.

TOPPINGS TO ADD BEFORE BAKING:

★ A crunchy sugar topping is easy and effective. Use coarse sugars such as granulated, demerara or crushed sugar lumps.

★ Chopped and flaked nuts can be sprinkled over muffins in the same way as sugar. Nuts brown during baking, so check towards the end of cooking time. If they have browned sufficiently, but the muffins aren't quite cooked, put a baking tray on the shelf above the muffins; this will help stop the nuts from browning further, while the muffins finish cooking.

★ Candy-coated chocolate buttons retain their bright colors when baked and look good scattered over the tops of muffins.

★ For a streusel topping, ideal for fruit muffins, rub 3 tablespoons cold cubed butter into ¼ cup all-purpose flour until the mixture resembles breadcrumbs. Stir in 2 tablespoons superfine or light brown sugar, then gently squeeze into a ball. Wrap and chill for 15 minutes, then coarsely grate before sprinkling over the muffin batter.

★ For a crumble topping, make in the same way as streusel topping but don't squeeze the dough together. Try adding other flavorings such as a pinch of ground cinnamon, chopped nuts, or rolled oats.

★ To give savory muffins an attractive finish, sprinkle them with a few sunflower seeds, poppy seeds, sesame seeds, rolled oats, or finely grated Parmesan.

★ For a savory crumble topping, rub 2 tablespoons butter into 3 tablespoons all-purpose flour, then stir in 2 tablespoons grated cheddar cheese.

TROUBLESHOOTING

Occasionally muffins don't turn out quite as you had hoped. Try to work out what went wrong and why, so you can avoid the same problem when you bake the next batch.

Q – *Although they look perfect on the outside, my muffins have "tunnels" of air in them when broken open. How can I avoid this?*

A – Quite simply, you're over-mixing the batter. Tunnels are caused by an excess of air bubbles in the mixture. Excessive stirring also develops the gluten in the flour, so the muffins will be tough. Next time, gently stir the dry and wet ingredients together until they are just combined. Stop mixing while the batter is still a bit lumpy.

Q – *Unfortunately I can't eat butter and would like to make muffins with oil instead. Is this possible?*

A – Yes, butter and oil are interchangeable in most recipes. Remember, though, that butter contains only about 80% fat, the other 20% being milk solids and water, so reduce the amount of oil very slightly and make up to the same amount with a dash of milk or water, e.g. if a recipe calls for 8 tablespoons of butter, use 7 tablespoons of oil and 1 tablespoon of milk or water. When choosing oil, sunflower or safflower oils are preferable for sweet muffins because they have a mild flavor, while for muffins containing nuts, peanut oil works well. The more distinctive flavor of olive oil is good for many savory muffin recipes.

Q – *Some recipes only make 9 or 10 muffins. I find my muffin pan warps when I don't fill all 12 cups with mixture, making them rise unevenly. What can I do?*
A – Even good-quality, heavy-weight muffin tins warp sometimes. You can prevent this by pouring some hot water into any empty muffin cups before baking – they should be about one-third full. The steam will help the muffins to rise as well.

Q – *My last batch of muffins were dry and tough. What did I do wrong?*
A – There are a couple of reasons why this may have happened. Firstly, when making muffins, the ratio of flour to liquid is vital, so always measure these carefully. Take care not to pack down the flour tightly, and scrape off the excess with the flat blade of a knife to ensure it's completely level. Another cause of tough, dry muffins is over-baking; they are ready as soon as the tops spring back when lightly pressed with a finger, or when a toothpick inserted into the middle comes out clean.

Q – *I'd like to make mini muffins instead of standard-sized ones from my favorite recipe. Is this possible?*
A – Most muffin recipes can be made into the muffin size of your choice. Generally speaking, you can make 3 mini muffins to every 1 standard-size muffin. A mini muffin pan holds about 2 tablespoons of batter per cup and a standard muffin pan about 8 tablespoons of batter per cup. Obviously, the smaller the muffin, the quicker it cooks, so you will have to adjust baking time. Most mini muffins take 10–12 minutes and standard ones 18–20 minutes.

Q – *My muffins are always slightly flat, even though I measure carefully and use fresh leavening agents. Could my oven be at fault?*
A – Temperature is one of the secrets to well-risen, domed muffins. Make sure that the oven is completely heated before you bake your muffins, and close the oven door as quickly as possible to keep the heat trapped. Try setting the oven temperature slightly higher initially, then lower it as soon as you've added the muffins. This extra heat will create a burst of steam to help raise the batter.

CHOCOLATE
MUFFINS

VANILLA CHOCOLATE CHIP Muffins

If you prefer, make mini muffins (this recipe makes 36 mini muffins). Freeze them to pop into lunchboxes, or keep them in an airtight container for quick pop-in-the-mouth snacks.

MAKES 12

2 cups self-rising flour
1 teaspoon baking powder
¼ cup butter
⅓ cup superfine sugar
Scant 1 cup milk or semi-sweet chocolate chips
2 eggs, lightly beaten
1 cup milk
1 teaspoon vanilla extract

MUFFIN TIP
For chunkier chocolate chip muffins, measure 1 cup from a bar/block of milk or semi-sweet chocolate, then cut it into small chunks using a sharp knife, and use the chopped chocolate instead of the chocolate chips.

1. Preheat the oven to 400°F. Grease a 12-cup muffin pan or line the cups with paper muffin cups.

2. Mix the flour and baking powder in a large bowl. Rub in the butter until the mixture resembles fine breadcrumbs. Stir in the sugar and chocolate chips.

3. In a separate bowl, mix together the eggs, milk, and vanilla extract, then pour the milk mixture all at once into the dry ingredients. Mix briefly until just combined.

4. Spoon the batter into the prepared muffin cups, dividing it evenly. Bake in the oven for 18–20 minutes, or until well risen, golden, and firm to the touch. Cool in the tin for 10 minutes, then turn out onto a wire rack. Serve warm or cold.

MARSHMALLOW, CHOC & COLA Muffins

Great for teenage parties and sleepovers, these chocolate muffins contain mini marshmallows. The cola not only flavors and sweetens the muffins, but the carbonation helps to lighten the batter.

MAKES 12

1³/₄ cups self-rising flour
2 tablespoons unsweetened cocoa powder
1 teaspoon baking powder
Pinch of salt
¹/₂ cup superfine sugar
1 egg, lightly beaten
6 tablespoons vegetable oil
²/₃ cup cola
³/₄ cup mini marshmallows

MUFFIN TIP
If mini marshmallows are not available, snip larger marshmallows into quarters using kitchen scissors dipped in powdered sugar.

1. Preheat the oven to 375°F. Grease a 12-cup muffin pan or line the cups with paper muffin cups.

2. Mix the flour, cocoa powder, baking powder, salt, and sugar in a large bowl. In a separate bowl, mix together the egg and vegetable oil. Add the cola (it will froth up, so make sure the container is large enough), then pour the cola mixture all at once into the dry ingredients and mix briefly until just combined.

3. Place a large spoonful of batter into each prepared muffin cup, then add three or four mini marshmallows, keeping them in the middle of the muffin. Spoon the remaining batter on top, dividing it evenly.

4. Bake in the oven for about 20 minutes, or until well risen and firm to the touch. Cool in the pan for 10 minutes, then turn out onto a wire rack. Serve warm or cold.

CHOCOLATE & BRANDY DESSERT Muffins

These dark chocolate muffins are served with a sweet and creamy white chocolate sauce.

MAKES 12

2 cups self-rising flour
1 teaspoon baking powder
$1/2$ cup unsweetened cocoa powder
1 cup superfine sugar
1 egg, lightly beaten
$3/4$ cup buttermilk
$1/2$ cup butter, melted
2 tablespoons brandy
Finely grated zest of 1 small orange
Fresh fruit, to serve
2 teaspoons powdered sugar, sifted,
   to decorate

FOR THE WHITE CHOCOLATE SAUCE
Generous 1 cup white chocolate,
   broken into squares
6 tablespoons heavy cream
4 tablespoons light cream

1. Preheat the oven to 375°F. Grease a 12-cup non-stick muffin pan.

2. For the muffins, mix the flour, baking powder, cocoa powder, and sugar in a large bowl. In a separate bowl, mix together the egg, buttermilk, melted butter, brandy, and orange zest. Add the wet ingredients to the dry ingredients and mix briefly until just combined.

3. Spoon the batter into the prepared muffin cups, dividing evenly. Bake in the oven for 18–20 minutes, or until well risen and firm to the touch. Cool in the pan for 5 minutes, then turn onto a wire rack to cool completely.

4. For the white chocolate sauce, melt the chocolate and 2 tablespoons of the double cream in a heat-proof bowl placed over a pan of hot, but not boiling, water. Stir until smooth. Add the remaining double cream and the single cream and stir until blended. Remove from the heat and whisk the chocolate sauce until smooth.

5. Place a chocolate muffin on a plate and top with fresh fruit. Pour over a little of the warm white chocolate sauce, letting it dribble down the sides. Repeat with the remaining muffins. Dust with sifted powdered sugar before serving.

RICH CHOCOLATE TRUFFLE MINI Muffins

MAKES 24

Scant 1 cup self-rising flour

3 tablespoons unsweetened cocoa powder

3/4 teaspoon baking powder

2 tablespoons butter

1/4 cup superfine sugar

1 egg, lightly beaten

Scant 1/2 cup milk

1 tablespoon heavy cream

1 teaspoon vanilla extract

1 teaspoon powdered sugar, to decorate

FOR THE CHOCOLATE GANACHE

Scant 1/2 cup semi-sweet or milk chocolate chips

5 tablespoons heavy cream

MUFFIN TIP
To shorten the time the ganache takes to thicken, chill it in the fridge, stirring the mixture occasionally.

1. Preheat the oven to 400°F. Grease two 12-cup mini muffin pans or one 24-cup mini muffin pan, or line the cups with paper mini muffin cups.

2. For the muffins, mix the flour, cocoa powder and baking powder in a large bowl. Rub in the butter until the mixture resembles fine breadcrumbs. Stir in the sugar.

3. In a separate small bowl, mix together the egg, milk, cream, and vanilla extract, then pour the egg mixture all at once into the dry ingredients and mix briefly until just combined.

4. Spoon the batter into the prepared muffin cups, dividing evenly. Bake in the oven for 8–10 minutes, or until well risen and firm to the touch. Cool in the pans for 5 minutes, then turn onto a wire rack to cool completely.

5. While the muffins are baking, make the chocolate ganache. Put the chocolate chips in a small bowl. Bring the cream to a boil in a small saucepan. Pour the hot cream over the chocolate chips and stir until melted and smooth. Leave for about 1 hour to cool and thicken.

6. When the ganache is the consistency of softened butter, beat it for a few seconds, then spread a swirl of ganache on top of each muffin. Lightly dust the muffins with sifted powdered sugar before serving.

WHITE CHOCOLATE & MACADAMIA NUT Muffins

These delicious moist chocolate muffins are studded with white chocolate and the king of nuts—macadamia nuts.

MAKES 12

Scant 1 cup semi-sweet chocolate, coarsely chopped
1½ cups all-purpose flour
¾ cup packed light brown sugar
2 tablespoons unsweetened cocoa powder
1 teaspoon baking powder
½ teaspoon salt
¾ cup buttermilk
2 eggs, lightly beaten
1½ teaspoons vanilla extract
1 cup white chocolate, chopped
¾ cup unsalted macadamia nuts, coarsely chopped

MUFFIN TIP
Use chopped pistachios, hazelnuts, or pecans instead of macadamia nuts, if you prefer. Use white chocolate chips instead of chopped white chocolate, if you like.

1. Preheat the oven to 400°F. Grease a 12-cup muffin pan or line the cups with paper muffin cups.

2. Melt the semi-sweet chocolate in a small heat-proof bowl placed over a pan of barely simmering water, stirring occasionally until melted and smooth; do not allow the bottom of the bowl to touch the water. Remove from the heat and set aside.

3. Mix the flour, sugar, cocoa powder, baking powder, and salt in a large bowl. In a separate bowl, mix together the buttermilk, eggs, and vanilla extract.

4. Add the buttermilk mixture and the melted chocolate mixture to the dry ingredients and mix briefly until just combined. Fold in the white chocolate and macadamia nuts.

5. Spoon the batter into the prepared muffin cups, dividing it evenly. Bake in the oven for about 20 minutes, or until well risen and firm to the touch. Cool in the pan for 5 minutes, then turn out onto a wire rack. Serve warm or cold.

CHOCOLATE CHIP CRUMBLE Muffins

These have a double dose of chocolate: the muffin mixture is packed with chocolate chips then generously topped with a chocolate crumble.

MUFFIN TIP
For chunkier chocolate muffins, use coarsely chopped semi-sweet or milk chocolate instead of chocolate chips.

MAKES **12**

1³/₄ cups self-rising flour
1 teaspoon baking powder
Pinch of salt
¹/₄ cup butter
¹/₂ cup light brown sugar
Scant 1 cup semi-sweet or milk
    chocolate chips
2 eggs, lightly beaten
1 cup milk
2 teaspoons vanilla extract

FOR THE CHOCOLATE CRUMBLE
TOPPING
¹/₃ cup all-purpose flour
1 tablespoon unsweetened
    cocoa powder
3 tablespoons butter
2 tablespoons superfine sugar

1. Preheat the oven to 400°F. Grease a 12-cup muffin pan or line the cups with paper muffin cups.

2. For the chocolate crumble topping, sift the flour and cocoa powder into a bowl. Rub in the butter until the mixture resembles coarse breadcrumbs, then stir in the sugar. Set aside.

3. For the muffins, mix the flour, baking powder, and salt in a large bowl. Rub in the butter until the mixture resembles fine breadcrumbs. Stir in the sugar and chocolate chips.

4. In a separate bowl, mix together the eggs, milk, and vanilla extract. Pour the milk mixture all at once into the dry ingredients and mix briefly until just combined.

5. Spoon the batter into the prepared muffin cups, dividing it evenly, then sprinkle the tops with the crumble topping. Bake in the oven for 18–20 minutes, or until well risen and firm to the touch. Cool in the pan for 5 minutes, then turn out onto a wire rack. Serve warm or cold.

DARK CHOCOLATE & GINGER Muffins

MAKES 10

1 generous cup semi-sweet
   chocolate, roughly chopped
6 tablespoons butter
2 cups self-rising flour
3/4 cup light brown sugar
3/4 teaspoon baking soda
Pinch of salt
2 ounces preserved stem ginger,
   drained and finely chopped
3/4 cup sour cream
3 tablespoons light corn syrup
1 egg, lightly beaten
2 teaspoons vanilla extract
Scant 1/2 cup white chocolate, broken
   into squares
Extra chopped preserved stem ginger,
   to decorate

MUFFIN TIP
*For a simple finish, dust
these muffins with a little
sifted powdered sugar and
unsweetened cocoa powder,
if you prefer.*

1. Preheat the oven to 400°F. Grease 10 cups of a 12-cup muffin pan or line 10 cups with paper muffin cups.

2. Melt the semi-sweet chocolate and butter together in a medium heat-proof bowl placed over a pan of barely simmering water, stirring occasionally until smooth. Remove from the heat and cool for a few minutes.

3. Mix the flour, sugar, baking soda, salt, and ginger in a large bowl. In a separate bowl, mix together the sour cream, light corn syrup, egg, and vanilla extract, then add the melted chocolate mixture and stir until blended. Add the wet ingredients to the dry ingredients and mix briefly until just combined.

4. Spoon the batter into the prepared muffin cups, dividing evenly. Bake in the oven for about 20 minutes, or until risen and firm to the touch. Cool in the pan for 10 minutes, then turn onto a wire rack to cool completely.

5. Melt the white chocolate in a small heat-proof bowl placed over a pan of barely simmering water, stirring occasionally until smooth. Spoon the melted white chocolate into a small greaseproof paper piping bag, snip off the end and pipe zig-zags of chocolate over the tops of the muffins. Scatter a few pieces of chopped ginger over each and leave to set before serving.

WHITE CHOCOLATE, LEMON & RASPBERRY Muffins

Small chunks of white chocolate, grated lemon zest, and fresh raspberries combine to create these really tasty muffins, ideal for a mid-morning or afternoon snack.

MAKES 12

2 cups self-rising flour
1 teaspoon baking powder
$1/4$ cup butter
$1/3$ cup superfine sugar
$2/3$ cup fresh raspberries
Scant 1 cup white chocolate, coarsely chopped
Finely grated zest of 1 lemon
2 eggs, lightly beaten
1 cup milk

1. Preheat the oven to 400°F. Grease a 12-cup muffin pan or line the cups with paper muffin cups.

2. Mix the flour and baking powder in a large bowl. Rub in the butter until the mixture resembles fine breadcrumbs. Stir in the sugar, raspberries, white chocolate and lemon zest.

3. In a separate bowl, mix together the eggs and milk, then pour the egg mixture all at once into the dry ingredients and mix briefly until just combined.

4. Spoon the batter into the prepared muffin cups, dividing it evenly. Bake in the oven for 18–20 minutes, or until well risen, golden and firm to the touch. Cool in the pan for 5 minutes, then turn out onto a wire rack. Serve warm or cold.

MUFFIN TIP
You can use frozen raspberries in this recipe if fresh are not available. You don't even need to thaw them first.

DOUBLE CHOCOLATE CHIP Muffins

These delicious muffins are for true chocolate lovers who just can't get enough chocolate. Serve them freshly baked and warm from the oven for a real chocolatey treat.

MAKES 12

2 cups all-purpose flour
1 cup light brown sugar
2 tablespoons unsweetened cocoa powder
2 teaspoons baking soda
$\frac{1}{2}$ teaspoon salt
$1\frac{1}{2}$ cups milk
6 tablespoons butter or margarine, melted
2 eggs, lightly beaten
Scant 1 cup semi-sweet chocolate chips

1. Preheat the oven to 400°F. Grease a 12-cup muffin pan or line the cups with paper muffin cups.

2. Mix the flour, sugar, cocoa powder, baking soda, and salt in a large bowl. In a separate bowl, mix together the milk, melted butter or margarine, and eggs.

3. Add the wet ingredients all at once to the dry ingredients and mix briefly until just combined. Fold in the chocolate chips.

4. Spoon the batter into the prepared muffin cups, dividing it evenly. Bake in the oven for about 20 minutes, or until well risen. Cool in the pan for 5 minutes, then turn out onto a wire rack. Serve warm or cold.

MINTED CHOCOLATE
Muffins

Ideal for St. Patrick's Day, these chocolate muffins have chocolate mints folded into the mixture and are topped with minty cream icing and pistachio nuts.

MAKES **10**

1³/₄ cups all-purpose flour

2 tablespoons unsweetened cocoa powder

2 teaspoons baking powder

¹/₂ teaspoon baking soda

¹/₂ cup light brown sugar

Scant 1 cup chocolate mints or mint-flavored chocolate, roughly chopped

1 egg, separated

Pinch of salt

7 tablespoons butter, melted

¹/₂ cup sour cream

¹/₂ cup milk

FOR THE MINT CREAM ICING

¹/₂ cup whipping cream

¹/₄ teaspoon peppermint extract

1–2 drops green food coloring

4 tablespoons superfine sugar

1 cup pistachio nuts, chopped

1. Preheat the oven to 400°F. Grease 10 cups of a 12-cup muffin pan or line 10 cups with paper muffin cups.

2. For the muffins, mix the flour, cocoa powder, baking powder, baking soda, sugar, and chocolate mints or mint-flavored chocolate in a large bowl.

3. Put the egg white and salt in a clean bowl and whisk until soft peaks form. In a separate bowl, mix together the egg yolk, melted butter, soured cream and milk. Pour the milk mixture all at once into the dry ingredients and mix briefly until almost combined. Add the whisked egg white and gently fold into the mixture until combined.

4. Spoon the batter into the prepared muffin cups, dividing evenly. Bake in the oven for 18–20 minutes, or until well risen and firm to the touch. Cool in the pan for 10 minutes, then turn onto a wire rack to cool completely.

5. To make the icing, whip the cream in a bowl until soft peaks form. Add the peppermint extract and a drop or two of green food coloring, then whisk in the sugar a spoonful at a time until the mixture is fairly stiff. Spoon or pipe the minted-cream icing on top of the muffins, then scatter over the pistachio nuts. Serve within 1 hour of icing.

CHOCOLATE MALT
Muffins

Malted milk powder adds a subtle flavor to these chocolate muffins. They make a delicious bed-time treat, served while still warm.

MAKES 10

1³/₄ cups self-rising flour

3 tablespoons unsweetened
   cocoa powder

2 tablespoons malted milk powder

1 teaspoon baking powder

¹/₄ teaspoon baking soda

¹/₂ teaspoon salt

¹/₂ cup superfine sugar

1 egg, lightly beaten

1 cup milk

2 teaspoons vanilla extract

6 tablespoons butter, melted

1. Preheat the oven to 375°F. Grease 10 cups of a 12-cup muffin pan or line 10 cups with paper muffin cups.

2. Mix the flour, cocoa powder, malted milk powder, baking powder, baking soda, salt and sugar in a large bowl. In a separate bowl, mix together the egg, milk, vanilla extract, and melted butter.

3. Add the wet ingredients all at once to the dry ingredients and mix briefly until just combined.

4. Spoon the batter into the prepared muffin cups, dividing it evenly. Bake in the oven for about 20 minutes, or until well risen and firm to the touch. Cool in the pan for 5 minutes, then turn out onto a wire rack. Serve warm or cold.

MUFFIN TIP
If you prefer, use 6 tablespoons of sunflower oil instead of the melted butter.

BANANA, WALNUT & CHOC-CHIP Muffins

These muffins are delicious served warm, when the chocolate and banana have that soft, melt-in-the-mouth quality.

MAKES 12

2 cups self-rising flour
2 tablespoons light brown sugar
$\frac{1}{2}$ cup walnuts, chopped
Generous $\frac{1}{2}$ cup chocolate chips
2 ripe bananas (about $\frac{1}{2}$ lb), peeled
3 tablespoons vegetable oil
2 eggs, lightly beaten
$\frac{1}{2}$ cup sour cream

1. Preheat the oven to 400°F. Grease a 12-cup muffin pan or line the cups with paper muffin cups.

2. Mix together the flour, sugar, walnuts, and chocolate chips in a large bowl. In a separate bowl, mash the bananas until fairly smooth, then stir in the vegetable oil, eggs, and sour cream.

3. Add the wet ingredients all at once to the dry ingredients, and mix briefly until just combined.

4. Spoon the batter into the prepared muffin cups, dividing it evenly. Bake in the oven for about 20 minutes, or until risen and golden. Cool in the pan for 10 minutes, then turn out onto a wire rack. Serve warm or cold.

BLACK FOREST Muffins

MAKES 10

Scant ¾ cup butter

⅔ cup superfine sugar

4 eggs, separated

1 teaspoon vanilla extract

Scant 1 cup all-purpose flour

1 ounce unsweetened cocoa powder

1 teaspoon baking powder

3 ounces morello cherries in syrup (in a jar), well-drained

FOR THE CHERRY SYRUP & DECORATION

2 tablespoons superfine sugar

2 tablespoons syrup from a jar of morello cherries

2 tablespoons kirsch or cherry liqueur

⅔ cup heavy or whipping cream

1 tablespoon powdered sugar

10 morello cherries

Chocolate curls, to decorate

1. Preheat the oven to 350°F. Grease 10 cups of a 12-cup muffin pan or line 10 cups with paper muffin cups.

2. For the muffins, melt the butter and sugar in a heavy-based saucepan over a very low heat. Bring the mixture to a gentle boil and cook for 2 minutes, stirring constantly. Remove the pan from the heat and leave to cool, then transfer the mixture to a large mixing bowl. Set aside.

3. Put the egg whites in a clean bowl and whisk until soft peaks form, then set aside. Stir the egg yolks and vanilla extract into the cooled butter and sugar, then sift over the flour, cocoa powder, and baking powder and gently fold in with the morello cherries. Fold in the whisked egg whites.

4. Spoon the batter into the prepared muffin cups, dividing it evenly. Bake in the oven for 15–18 minutes, or until well risen and firm to the touch. Cool in the pan for 5 minutes, then transfer to a wire rack.

5. Meanwhile, make the syrup. Gently heat the superfine sugar and morello cherry syrup in a small saucepan, stirring until the sugar has dissolved. Remove the pan from the heat and stir in 1 tablespoon of the kirsch or cherry liqueur. Drizzle a little syrup over the top of each warm muffin.

6. Whip the cream in a bowl with the remaining kirsch or cherry liqueur and the powdered sugar until soft peaks form, then spoon the mixture into a piping bag fitted with a large star tip. Pipe a swirl of flavored cream on top of each cooled muffin and decorate with a morello cherry and a few chocolate curls. Chill until ready to serve.

CHOCOLATE-FILLED
Muffins

These hazelnut-topped muffins hide a delicious rich chocolate center to create a tempting sweet treat.

MAKES **12**

2 cups self-rising flour
1 teaspoon baking powder
$^1/_4$ cup butter
Generous $^1/_3$ cup superfine sugar
2 eggs, lightly beaten
1 cup milk
1 teaspoon vanilla extract
2 tablespoons finely chopped
    hazelnuts
1 tablespoon demerara sugar

FOR THE FILLING

$1^1/_2$ tablespoons butter, softened
$^2/_3$ cup powdered sugar
$1^1/_2$ teaspoons milk
$^1/_2$ teaspoon vanilla extract
2 ounces semi-sweet chocolate,
    melted

1. Preheat the oven to 400°F. Grease a 12-cup muffin pan or line the cups with paper muffin cups.

2. For the filling, cream the butter in a small bowl. Gradually add the powdered sugar, beating until well mixed. Beat in the milk, vanilla extract, and melted chocolate until well combined. Set aside.

3. For the muffins, mix the flour and baking powder in a large bowl. Rub in the butter until the mixture resembles fine breadcrumbs. Stir in the superfine sugar. In a separate bowl, mix together the eggs, milk, and vanilla extract. Pour the egg mixture all at once into the dry ingredients and mix briefly until just combined.

4. Put a spoonful of the batter into each prepared muffin cup. Drop a large teaspoonful of the filling mixture on top of each, then cover with the remaining muffin batter, dividing it evenly.

5. Mix together the chopped hazelnuts and demerara sugar and sprinkle this mixture evenly over the tops of the muffins.

6. Bake in the oven for 18–20 minutes, or until well risen, golden and firm to the touch. Cool in the pan for 5 minutes, then turn out onto a wire rack. These muffins are best served warm.

CAPPUCCINO Muffins

Don't be tempted to substitute instant coffee for ground coffee in this recipe.
If possible, use a rich, dark roasted variety of coffee for the best flavor.

MAKES 12

³/₄ cup self-rising flour
1¹/₄ cups all-purpose flour
1 tablespoon baking powder
¹/₂ teaspoon salt
²/₃ cup unsweetened cocoa powder
¹/₂ cup light brown sugar
2 tablespoons finely ground coffee
6 tablespoons butter, softened
1 cup sour cream
1 cup whipping cream
2 eggs, lightly beaten
Finely grated zest of 2 oranges
4 ounces dark bitter chocolate,
    coarsely chopped

1. Preheat the oven to 350°F. Grease a 12-cup muffin pan or line the cups with paper muffin cups.

2. Mix the flours, baking powder, salt, and cocoa powder in a large bowl. Stir in the sugar and ground coffee.

3. In a separate bowl, beat together the butter, sour cream, whipping cream, and eggs. Add the wet ingredients to the dry ingredients along with the orange zest and chocolate and mix until just combined.

4. Spoon the batter into the prepared muffin cups, dividing it evenly. Bake in the oven for 15–20 minutes, or until risen and firm to the touch. Cool in the pan for 10 minutes, then turn out onto a wire rack. Serve warm or cold.

SPECKLED CHOCOLATE Muffins

These muffins contain oats soaked in vanilla-flavored milk, which gives them a lovely texture. The speckled appearance is achieved by stirring coarsely grated or finely chopped chocolate into the mixture.

MAKES 10

1/2 cup rolled oats
1 1/4 cups milk
2 teaspoons vanilla extract
1 3/4 cups all-purpose flour
1 tablespoon baking powder
1/2 teaspoon salt
1/2 cup superfine sugar
Scant 1 cup semi-sweet chocolate, coarsely grated or very finely chopped
1 egg, lightly beaten
1/2 cup butter, melted

1. Preheat the oven to 400°F. Grease 10 cups of a 12-cup muffin pan or line 10 cups with paper muffin cups.

2. Put the oats in a bowl and pour over the milk and vanilla extract. Stir, then leave to soak while you prepare the remaining ingredients.

3. Mix the flour, baking powder, salt, and sugar in a large bowl. Stir in the chocolate. Stir the egg and melted butter into the soaked oat mixture. Add the oat mixture all at once to the dry ingredients and mix briefly until just combined.

4. Spoon the batter into the prepared muffin cups, dividing it evenly. Bake in the oven for 18–20 minutes, or until risen and golden. Cool in the pan for 10 minutes, then turn out onto a wire rack. Serve warm or cold.

MUFFIN TIP
A mixture of semi-sweet, milk, and white chocolate can be used to give the muffins a marbled effect.

GLAZED MOCHA CHOC-CHIP Muffins

MAKES 12

2 cups self-rising flour
1 teaspoon baking powder
¼ cup butter
Generous ⅓ cup sugar
Scant 1 cup semi-sweet chocolate chips or semi-sweet chocolate, chopped
2 eggs, lightly beaten
⅔ cup milk
5 tablespoons fresh espresso coffee, cooled

FOR THE CHOCOLATE GLAZE

2 tablespoons butter
2 tablespoons unsweetened cocoa powder
2 tablespoons fresh espresso, cooled
1¼ cups powdered sugar, sifted
½ teaspoon vanilla extract

1. Preheat the oven to 400°F. Grease a 12-cup muffin pan or line the cups with paper muffin cups.

2. For the muffins, mix the flour and baking powder in a large bowl. Rub in the butter until the mixture resembles fine breadcrumbs. Stir in the sugar and chocolate chips or chopped chocolate. In a separate bowl, mix together the eggs, milk, and espresso. Pour this mixture all at once into the dry ingredients and mix briefly until just combined.

3. Spoon the batter into the prepared muffin cups, dividing it evenly. Bake in the oven for 18–20 minutes, or until well risen and firm to the touch. Cool in the pan for 5 minutes, then turn out onto a wire rack and leave to cool completely.

4. For the chocolate glaze, melt the butter in a small saucepan over a low heat. Add the cocoa powder and espresso coffee, stirring constantly until the mixture thickens; do not boil. Remove the pan from the heat and slowly add the powdered sugar and vanilla extract, beating until smooth. If necessary, thin the glaze with a little hot water until it is thin enough to drizzle over the cooled muffins. Leave the glazed muffins to stand for about 30 minutes, or until set, before serving.

TRIPLE CHOCOLATE CHUNK Muffins

These chocolate-packed muffins are given a lighter touch by folding whisked egg white into the mixture before baking.

MAKES 10

1³/₄ cups all-purpose flour
2 teaspoons baking powder
¹/₂ teaspoon baking soda
¹/₂ cup light brown sugar
2 ounces semi-sweet chocolate, roughly chopped
2 ounces milk chocolate, roughly chopped
2 ounces white chocolate, roughly chopped
1 egg, separated
¹/₄ teaspoon salt
7 tablespoons butter, melted
¹/₄ cup sour cream
³/₄ cup milk
1 teaspoon vanilla extract

1. Preheat the oven to 400°F. Grease 10 cups of a 12-cup muffin pan or line 10 cups with paper muffin cups.

2. Mix the flour, baking powder, baking soda, sugar, and about two-thirds of each type of chocolate in a large bowl.

3. Put the egg white and salt in a clean bowl and whisk until soft peaks form. In a separate bowl, mix together the egg yolk, melted butter, sour cream, milk, and vanilla extract. Pour the milk mixture all at once into the dry ingredients and mix briefly until almost combined. Add the whisked egg white and gently fold into the mixture until combined.

4. Spoon the batter into the prepared muffin cups, dividing it evenly, then gently press the remaining mixed chocolate on top of the muffins. Bake in the oven for 18–20 minutes, or until well risen and firm to the touch. Cool in the pan for 10 minutes, then turn out onto a wire rack. Serve warm or cold.

MUFFIN TIP
If you prefer, use just one or two types of chocolate. Flavored chocolates, such as orange, mint, or hazelnut varieties, would also work well.

CHOCOLATE RUM & RAISIN Muffins

If time allows, soak the raisins in rum overnight so that they are really plump and well-flavored.

MAKES **10**

1 cup raisins
2 tablespoons dark rum
1¾ cups all-purpose flour
3 tablespoons unsweetened cocoa powder
1 tablespoon baking powder
Pinch of salt
Pinch of freshly grated nutmeg
Scant ¾ cup superfine sugar
Scant 1 cup semi-sweet chocolate, coarsely chopped
1 egg, lightly beaten
⅔ cup milk
6 tablespoons vegetable oil

1. Put the raisins in a small bowl, pour over the rum, and stir to coat. Cover and leave to soak for at least 15 minutes. Preheat the oven to 375°F. Grease 10 cups of a 12-cup muffin pan or line 10 cups with paper muffin cups.

2. Mix the flour, cocoa powder, baking powder, salt, nutmeg, sugar, and chocolate in a large bowl. In a separate bowl, mix together the egg, milk, vegetable oil, and rum-soaked raisins. Add the raisin mixture all at once to the dry ingredients and mix briefly until just combined.

3. Spoon the batter into the prepared muffin cups, dividing it evenly. Bake in the oven for about 20 minutes, or until risen and firm to the touch. Cool in the pan for 10 minutes, then turn out onto a wire rack. Serve warm or cold.

MUFFIN TIP
If you prefer, use an orange-flavored liqueur instead of the rum, or simply soak the raisins in fruit juice.

CHOCOLATE ALMOND Muffins

These rich chocolate muffins are studded with small pieces of marzipan, keeping their texture soft and moist. A scattering of flaked almonds gives them a lavish finish.

MAKES 12

1½ cups self-rising flour
3 tablespoons unsweetened cocoa powder
1 teaspoon baking powder
Pinch of salt
¼ cup butter
½ cup superfine sugar
½ cup marzipan, cut into small cubes
2 eggs, lightly beaten
1 cup milk
¼ teaspoon almond extract
¼ cup flaked almonds

1. Preheat the oven to 375°F. Grease a 12-cup muffin pan or line the cups with paper muffin cups.

2. Mix the flour, cocoa powder, baking powder, and salt in a large bowl. Rub in the butter until the mixture resembles fine breadcrumbs. Stir in the sugar and marzipan.

3. In a separate bowl, mix together the eggs, milk, and almond extract. Pour the milk mixture all at once into the dry ingredients and mix briefly until just combined.

4. Spoon the batter into the prepared muffin cups, dividing it evenly, then sprinkle the tops with flaked almonds. Bake in the oven for about 20 minutes, or until well risen and firm to the touch. Cool in the pan for 10 minutes, then turn out onto a wire rack. Serve warm or cold.

MUFFIN TIP

Instead of flaked almonds, scatter ½ cup coarsely grated marzipan over the tops of the muffins before baking. Cover the muffins with foil after 12 minutes baking time to prevent the marzipan from over-browning.

CHOCOLATE FUDGE
Muffins

These delicious muffins pack a real chocolate
punch and are definitely not for the faint-hearted.

MAKES 12

Scant 1 cup semi-sweet chocolate,
    coarsely chopped
2 ounces dark bitter chocolate,
    coarsely chopped
6 tablespoons butter
2 cups all-purpose flour
¾ cup light brown sugar
1 teaspoon baking soda
¼ teaspoon salt
¾ cup sour cream
3 tablespoons light corn syrup
1 egg, lightly beaten
1¼ teaspoons vanilla extract
Generous ½ cup semi-sweet
    chocolate chips

1. Preheat the oven to 400°F. Grease a 12-cup muffin pan or line the cups with paper muffin cups.

2. Melt the semi-sweet chocolate, bitter chocolate, and butter together in a heat-proof bowl placed over a pan of barely simmering water, stirring occasionally until smooth. Remove from the heat and cool slightly.

3. Mix the flour, sugar, baking soda, and salt in a large bowl. In a separate small bowl, mix together the sour cream, corn syrup, egg, and vanilla extract, then fold this into the melted chocolate mixture. Fold in the chocolate chips. Add the chocolate mixture to the dry ingredients, mixing briefly until just combined.

4. Spoon the batter into the prepared muffin cups, dividing it evenly. Bake in the oven for about 20 minutes, or until well risen and firm to the touch. Cool in the pan for 5 minutes, then turn out onto a wire rack. Serve warm or cold.

MUFFIN TIP
Dark bitter chocolate with a cocoa solids content of 70% (minimum) would work well in this recipe.

CHOCOLATE CHIP & ORANGE Muffins

The orange zest adds a lovely freshness to these muffins, for those who may otherwise find chocolate muffins a little too rich.

MAKES 12

2 cups all-purpose flour
1 cup light brown sugar
2 tablespoons unsweetened cocoa powder
2 teaspoons baking soda
$\frac{1}{2}$ teaspoon salt
Generous $\frac{1}{2}$ cup semi-sweet chocolate chips
1 cup milk
6 tablespoons butter or margarine, melted
2 eggs, lightly beaten
Finely grated zest of 1 orange

1. Preheat the oven to 400°F. Grease a 12-cup muffin pan or line the cups with paper muffin cups.

2. Mix the flour, sugar, cocoa powder, baking soda, salt and chocolate chips in a large bowl.

3. In a separate bowl, mix together the milk, melted butter or margarine, eggs, and orange zest. Add the wet ingredients to the dry ingredients and mix briefly until just combined.

4. Spoon the batter into the prepared muffin cups, dividing it evenly. Bake in the oven for about 20 minutes, or until well risen and firm to the touch. Cool in the pan for 5 minutes, then turn out onto a wire rack. Serve warm or cold.

CHOCOLATE CHEESECAKE
Muffins

A delicious cheesecake topping mixture is swirled into the muffin batter to create these decadent almond-topped chocolate muffins.

MAKES 12

1 cup all-purpose flour
Generous ¾ cup superfine sugar
⅓ cup unsweetened cocoa powder
½ teaspoon baking soda
¼ teaspoon salt
½ cup sour cream
3 tablespoons vegetable oil
¼ cup butter, melted and cooled
2 eggs, lightly beaten
1 teaspoon vanilla extract
3 ounces semi-sweet chocolate, melted
⅓ cup flaked almonds
FOR THE CHEESECAKE MIXTURE
Generous ¾ cup cream cheese, at room temperature
Generous ¼ cup superfine sugar
1 egg, lightly beaten
⅛ teaspoon vanilla extract

1. Preheat the oven to 375°F. Grease a 12-cup muffin pan or line the cups with paper muffin cups.

2. For the cheesecake mixture, combine the cream cheese, sugar, egg, and vanilla extract in a bowl. Set aside.

3. For the muffins, mix the flour, sugar, cocoa powder, baking soda, and salt in a large bowl. In a separate bowl, mix together the sour cream, vegetable oil, melted butter, eggs, vanilla extract, and melted chocolate. Add the wet ingredients to the dry ingredients and mix briefly until just combined.

4. Spoon the batter into the prepared muffin cups, dividing it evenly, then carefully spoon a little of the cheesecake mixture over the chocolate batter in each muffin cup. Swirl the mixture slightly with a knife so the batter appears marbled. Sprinkle the tops with flaked almonds.

5. Bake in the oven for 20–25 minutes, or until risen and firm to the touch. Cool in the pan for 5 minutes, then turn out onto a wire rack. Serve warm or cold.

FRUIT
MUFFINS

PEAR & WALNUT Muffins with Butterscotch Sauce

These lightly spiced fruit and nut muffins, drizzled with butterscotch sauce, create a wonderful dessert or sweet treat.

MAKES 12

2 cups all-purpose flour
2 teaspoons baking powder
$1/2$ teaspoon baking soda
1 cup superfine sugar
$1/4$ teaspoon salt
1 teaspoon ground cinnamon
1 teaspoon ground cardamom
2 eggs, lightly beaten
$3/4$ cup sour cream
$3/4$ cup butter, melted
3 canned pear halves in fruit juice, drained and diced
$1/2$ cup walnuts, coarsely chopped

FOR THE BUTTERSCOTCH SAUCE

1 cup dark brown sugar
$1/2$ cup butter
4 tablespoons whipping cream

1. Preheat the oven to 400°F. Grease a 12-cup muffin pan or line the cups with paper muffin cups.

2. For the muffins, mix the flour, baking powder, baking soda, sugar, salt, cinnamon, and cardamom in a large bowl.

3. In a separate bowl, whisk together the eggs, sour cream, and melted butter. Add the wet ingredients to the dry ingredients along with the pears and walnuts and mix briefly until just combined.

4. Spoon the batter into the prepared muffin cups, dividing it evenly. Bake in the oven for about 20 minutes, or until risen and golden.

5. Meanwhile, for the butterscotch sauce, combine the sugar and butter in a saucepan and place over low heat until the butter has melted and sugar has dissolved, stirring occasionally; do not allow the mixture to boil. Remove the pan from the heat and add the cream. Mix well and keep warm.

6. When the muffins are baked, cool them in the pan for 10 minutes, then turn onto a wire rack. Serve warm drizzled with the butterscotch sauce.

MARMALADE MORNING Muffins

Perfect for breakfast, these marmalade-flavored muffins are made with whole-wheat flour, sunflower margarine, and juicy chunks of fresh pear, making them a healthy start to the day.

MAKES 12

½ cup whole-wheat flour
1½ cups all-purpose white flour
¾ cup unrefined superfine sugar
1 tablespoon baking powder
½ teaspoon salt
2 eggs, lightly beaten
2 tablespoons orange marmalade
¾ cup unsweetened orange juice
½ cup sunflower margarine, melted
2 medium ripe pears, peeled, cored and chopped

FOR THE TOPPING

1 tablespoon unsweetened orange juice
4 tablespoons orange marmalade

1. Preheat the oven to 400°F. Grease a 12-cup muffin pan or line the cups with paper muffin cups.

2. For the muffins, mix the flours, sugar, baking powder, and salt in a large bowl. In a separate bowl, mix together the eggs, marmalade, orange juice, melted margarine, and two-thirds of the chopped pears. Add the wet ingredients to the dry ingredients, mixing briefly until just combined.

3. Spoon the batter into the prepared muffin cups, dividing it evenly. Scatter with the remaining chopped pears, pressing the pieces gently into the batter. Bake in the oven for about 20 minutes, or until risen and golden. Cool in the pan for 5 minutes, then turn out onto a wire rack.

4. Meanwhile, for the topping, gently heat the orange juice and marmalade together in a small saucepan, stirring occasionally until melted and combined. Spoon and brush over the tops of the warm muffins. Serve warm.

OVERNIGHT Muffins

This fruity muffin mixture improves if left for at least 8 hours or overnight in the fridge. It's therefore ideal for making brunch-time muffins or for days when you know you'll be really busy.

MAKES 12

1½ cups all-purpose flour

½ cup oat bran

1 cup unsweetened muesli

½ cup light brown sugar

1½ teaspoons ground cinnamon

1 teaspoon baking soda

¾ cup dried apricots or dried dates, chopped

1 egg, lightly beaten

1½ cups buttermilk

½ cup vegetable oil

2 tablespoons demerara sugar, to decorate

1. Mix the flour, oat bran, muesli, brown sugar, cinnamon, baking soda, and dried apricots or dates in a large bowl. In a separate bowl, mix together the egg, buttermilk, and vegetable oil.

2. Pour the wet ingredients into the dry ingredients and mix briefly until just combined. Cover the bowl with plastic wrap and refrigerate for at least 8 hours, or overnight.

3. When ready to bake, preheat the oven to 375°F. Grease a 12-cup muffin pan or line the cups with paper muffin cups.

4. Spoon the batter into the prepared muffin cups, dividing it evenly. Sprinkle the demerara sugar evenly over the tops of the muffins. Bake in the oven for about 20 minutes, or until risen and firm. Cool in the pan for 10 minutes, then turn out onto a wire rack. Serve warm or cold.

MUFFIN TIP

Experiment by using your favorite dried fruit in the muffins; cranberries, blueberries, and chopped tropical fruits would all work well.

MIXED BERRY Muffins

If fresh berries are not available, you can use frozen berries in this recipe; there's no need to thaw them first.

MAKES 12

2 cups self-rising flour
1 teaspoon baking powder
²/₃ cup superfine sugar
²/₃ cup white chocolate, finely chopped
²/₃ cup fresh raspberries
1 cup fresh blueberries
1 egg, lightly beaten
¹/₂ cup butter, melted
³/₄ cup buttermilk
3 tablespoons milk
1 teaspoon vanilla extract
2 teaspoons powdered sugar, to decorate

1. Preheat the oven to 400°F. Grease a 12-cup muffin pan or line the cups with paper muffin cups.

2. Mix the flour, baking powder, sugar, and chocolate in a large bowl. Sprinkle two-thirds each of the raspberries and blueberries over the dry ingredients.

3. In a separate bowl, mix together the egg, melted butter, buttermilk, milk, and vanilla extract. Add the buttermilk mixture all at once to the dry ingredients and mix briefly until just combined.

4. Spoon the batter into the prepared muffin cups, dividing it evenly, then top with the remaining berries, pressing them gently into the batter. Bake in the oven for about 20 minutes, or until risen and golden. Cool in the pan for 10 minutes, then turn out onto a wire rack. Serve warm or cold, dusted with sifted powdered sugar.

MUFFIN TIP
If buttermilk is unavailable, stir 1 teaspoon of lemon juice or white vinegar into ³/₄ cup low fat milk and leave to stand for about 1 hour before using.

MUESLI-TOPPED APPLE SAUCE Muffins

Using ready-made apple sauce and muesli means that these muffins are quick and easy to make, but you can of course prepare either, or both, yourself if you prefer.

MAKES 12

2 cups all-purpose flour
$\frac{1}{2}$ cup light brown sugar
1 tablespoon baking powder
$\frac{1}{2}$ teaspoon baking soda
$\frac{1}{2}$ teaspoon salt
$\frac{1}{2}$ teaspoon ground cinnamon
$\frac{1}{2}$ teaspoon freshly grated nutmeg
$\frac{1}{4}$ cup butter, melted
$1\frac{1}{3}$ cups apple sauce
$\frac{1}{4}$ cup milk
1 egg, lightly beaten
$\frac{1}{2}$ cup unsweetened muesli

1. Preheat the oven to 425°F. Grease a 12-cup muffin pan or line the cups with paper muffin cups.

2. Mix the flour, sugar, baking powder, baking soda, salt, cinnamon, and nutmeg in a large bowl. In a separate bowl, mix together the melted butter, apple sauce, milk, and egg. Add the wet ingredients to the dry ingredients and mix briefly until just combined. Spoon the batter into the prepared muffin cups, dividing it evenly.

3. Place the muesli in a bowl and crush lightly, using the back of a spoon or the end of a rolling pin, until the pieces are small and even. Sprinkle the crushed muesli evenly over the muffins.

4. Bake in the oven for 15–20 minutes, or until risen and golden. Cool in the pan for 10 minutes, then turn out onto a wire rack. Serve warm or cold.

MUFFIN TIP
Use a muesli with raisins or other dried fruit and nuts for added crunch and sweetness, but make sure that it is unsweetened.

RASPBERRY CHEESECAKE
Muffins

MAKES 12

FOR THE CHEESECAKE MIXTURE
$^2/_3$ cup cream cheese, softened
$^3/_4$ cup sugar
1 egg
$^1/_2$ teaspoon vanilla extract

FOR THE MUFFINS
1 cup milk
6 tablespoons butter
1 teaspoon vanilla extract
2 eggs, lightly beaten
1$^1/_2$ cups all-purpose flour
$^1/_2$ cup superfine sugar
2 teaspoons baking powder
$^1/_2$ teaspoon salt
$^2/_3$ cup fresh or frozen raspberries

1. Preheat the oven to 400°F. Grease a 12-cup muffin pan or line the cups with paper muffin cups.

2. For the cheesecake mixture, combine the cream cheese, sugar, egg, and vanilla extract in a bowl, mixing well. Set aside.

3. For the muffins, combine the milk, butter, and vanilla extract in a saucepan and heat gently, stirring, until the butter is melted. Remove the pan from the heat and allow to cool. Beat in the eggs.

4. Mix the flour, sugar, baking powder, and salt in a large bowl. Add the milk mixture to the dry ingredients and mix briefly until just combined. Gently fold in the raspberries.

5. Spoon the batter into the prepared muffin cups, dividing it evenly. Top each muffin with 2 teaspoons of the cream cheese mixture and swirl slightly with a knife. Bake in the oven for about 20 minutes, or until the tops spring back when lightly touched. Cool in the pan for 10 minutes, then turn out onto a wire rack. Serve warm or cold.

CRANBERRY & PECAN
Muffins

These cinnamon-spiced muffins would also be very tasty with juicy raisins
in place of the cranberries, if you prefer.

MAKES **12**

2 cups all-purpose flour
1/2 cup light brown sugar
1/4 cup sugar
2 teaspoons baking powder
1 teaspoon salt
1 teaspoon ground cinnamon
1 1/4 cups milk
1/2 cup vegetable oil
1 egg, lightly beaten
1 cup dried cranberries
1/3 cup pecans, chopped

1. Preheat the oven to 350°F. Grease a 12-cup muffin pan or line the
cups with paper muffin cups.

2. Combine the flour, sugars, baking powder, salt, and cinnamon in a bowl.
In a separate bowl, mix together the milk, vegetable oil, and egg.

3. Add the wet ingredients to the dry ingredients, mixing briefly until
just combined. Gently fold in the cranberries and pecans.

4. Spoon the batter into the prepared muffin cups, dividing it evenly.
Bake in the oven for about 25 minutes, or until risen and golden. Cool in
the pan for 5 minutes, then turn out onto a wire rack. Serve warm or cold.

MUFFIN TIP
*Use ground pumpkin
pie spice or ground
ginger in place of ground
cinnamon for a tasty
alternative.*

APRICOT, VANILLA & LEMON Muffins

These are classy muffins, with a beautiful fresh vanilla fragrance. They are delicious served warm for a mid-morning snack or an afternoon treat.

MAKES 12

1/2 vanilla bean
1 cup superfine sugar
2 cups all-purpose flour
1 tablespoon baking powder
3/4 teaspoon salt
1/2 cup butter, diced
1/2 cup dried apricots, chopped
Finely grated zest of 1 lemon
1 egg, lightly beaten
1 cup milk

MUFFIN TIP
If you don't have a vanilla bean, add 1 teaspoon of good quality vanilla extract to the wet ingredients, and add the sugar to the dry ingredients.

1. Preheat the oven to 400°F. Grease a 12-cup muffin pan or line the cups with paper muffin cups.

2. Put the vanilla bean and sugar into a blender or food processor and blend until the vanilla bean is very finely chopped. Mix the flour, baking powder, and salt in a large bowl, then stir in the vanilla sugar. Rub in the butter until the mixture resembles fine breadcrumbs. Stir in the dried apricots and lemon zest.

3. In a separate small bowl, combine the egg and milk, then add this to the flour mixture, mixing briefly until just combined.

4. Spoon the batter into the prepared muffin cups, dividing it evenly. Bake in the oven for about 20 minutes, or until risen and golden. Cool in the pan for 10 minutes, then turn out onto a wire rack. Serve warm or cold.

RUM-GLAZED CARIBBEAN Muffins

Use your favorite tropical fruits for these muffins; pineapple, papaya, and mango make a great combination.

MAKES 10

2 cups all-purpose flour
2 1/2 teaspoons baking powder
1/4 cup sugar
1/2 cup light brown sugar
1/2 teaspoon salt
1/2 cup flaked coconut
1 cup ready-to-eat mixed dried tropical fruit, finely chopped
Scant 1 1/4 cups milk
1/2 cup vegetable oil
1 egg, lightly beaten

FOR THE ICING
3/4 cup powdered sugar
1 tablespoon white rum

1. Preheat the oven to 375°F. Grease 10 cups of a 12-cup muffin pan or line 10 cups with paper muffin cups.

2. For the muffins, mix the flour, baking powder, sugars, salt, coconut, and 2/3 cup of the tropical fruit in a large bowl. In a separate bowl, combine the milk, vegetable oil, and egg. Add the wet ingredients to the dry ingredients, mixing briefly until just combined.

3. Spoon the batter into the prepared muffin cups, dividing it evenly. Bake in the oven for about 20 minutes, or until risen and golden. Cool in the pan for 5 minutes, then turn onto a wire rack to cool completely.

4. For the icing, sift the powdered sugar into a bowl and gradually blend in the rum until you have a smooth icing. Drizzle the rum icing evenly over the tops of the muffins, then sprinkle with the remaining chopped tropical fruit to serve.

MUFFIN TIP
If you prefer, make the icing with tropical fruit juice or orange juice instead of the rum. Flaked coconut is available from many health food shops, but use desiccated coconut if you can't find flaked coconut.

MINI ICED CHERRY Muffins

These dainty mini muffins have a fudgy icing, colored and flavored with morello cherry syrup.

MAKES 24

1 cup self-rising flour
¾ teaspoon baking powder
2 tablespoons butter
3 tablespoons superfine sugar
6 morello cherries (jarred), drained and finely chopped
1 egg, lightly beaten
½ cup milk
1 teaspoon vanilla extract
12 morello cherries (jarred), drained and halved, to decorate

FOR THE ICING

Scant ⅔ cup superfine sugar
1½ teaspoons unsalted butter, at room temperature
1 teaspoon syrup from a jar of morello cherries (optional)
3 teaspoons cold water

1. Preheat the oven to 375°F. Line two 12-cup mini muffin pans or one 24-cup mini muffin pan with paper mini muffin cups.

2. For the muffins, mix the flour and baking powder in a large bowl. Rub in the butter until the mixture resembles fine breadcrumbs. Stir in the sugar and morello cherries. In a separate bowl, mix together the egg, milk, and vanilla extract. Pour the wet mixture all at once into the dry ingredients and mix briefly until just combined.

3. Spoon the batter into the prepared muffin cups, dividing it evenly. Bake in the oven for about 10 minutes, or until well risen and firm to the touch. Cool in the pans for 5 minutes, then turn out onto a wire rack. Leave to cool completely.

4. For the icing, sift the powdered sugar into a small bowl; set aside. Gently heat the butter, cherry syrup (if using), and water in a small saucepan until the butter has melted, stirring. Pour onto the powdered sugar and stir until smooth. Carefully spoon the icing over the muffins and top each with half a morello cherry. Leave to set before serving.

RED & ORANGE
Muffins

This classic combination is enhanced with chopped pecans to give a satisfying crunch and texture.

MAKES 12

2 cups all-purpose flour

1 cup superfine sugar

1 tablespoon baking powder

1/2 teaspoon salt

3/4 cup fresh or frozen cranberries (thawed if frozen), coarsely chopped

Finely grated zest of 1 orange

2 tablespoons chopped pecans

1 egg, lightly beaten

1 cup milk

3 tablespoons butter, melted

1. Preheat the oven to 400°F. Grease a 12-cup muffin pan or line the cups with paper muffin cups.

2. Mix the flour, sugar, baking powder, and salt in a large bowl. Stir in the cranberries, orange zest, and pecans.

3. In a separate bowl, mix together the egg, milk, and melted butter. Add the wet ingredients to the dry ingredients and mix briefly until just combined.

4. Spoon the batter into the prepared muffin cups, dividing it evenly. Bake in the oven for about 20 minutes, or until risen and golden. Cool in the pan for 10 minutes, then turn out onto a wire rack. Serve warm or cold.

MUFFIN TIP
Fresh blueberries instead of the cranberries and walnuts instead of the pecans would also work well in this recipe.

HAPPY BIRTHDAY Muffins

Lemon-flavored muffins are split in half and sandwiched with jelly. Drizzled with glacé icing, decorated with sprinkles or small candies, and topped with a birthday candle, they make a great alternative to a traditional birthday cake.

MAKES **10**

1³/₄ cups self-rising flour
1 teaspoon baking powder
²/₃ cup superfine sugar
Pinch of salt
Finely grated zest of 1 lemon
1 egg, lightly beaten
²/₃ cup milk
6 tablespoons butter, melted

FOR THE FILLING & ICING

4 ounces seedless raspberry jelly
   (about 6 heaping tablespoons)
1¹/₂ cups powdered sugar
2–3 tablespoons lemon juice
Sprinkles or small candies,
   to decorate

MUFFIN TIP
If you prefer, fill the muffins with lemon curd or chocolate spread instead of jelly.

1. Preheat the oven to 375°F. Grease 10 cups of a 12-cup non-stick muffin pan.

2. For the muffins, mix the flour, baking powder, sugar, salt, and lemon zest in a large bowl. In a separate bowl, mix together the egg, milk, and melted butter. Add the wet ingredients all at once to the dry ingredients, and mix briefly until just combined.

3. Spoon the batter into the prepared muffin cups, dividing it evenly. Bake in the oven for about 20 minutes, or until well risen and golden brown. Cool in the pan for 5 minutes, then turn out onto a wire rack and leave to cool completely.

4. When the muffins are cold, split them in half horizontally, then sandwich them back together with the jelly. Sift the powdered sugar into a small bowl and add enough lemon juice to make a smooth, thick icing. Drizzle or spread the icing over the tops of the muffins, then decorate with sprinkles or small candies. Leave to set before serving.

FRESH RASPBERRY & LEMON Muffins

These refreshing fresh fruit muffins have a slightly rounded rather than a peaked top and a light sponge-like texture. If lemon-flavored yogurt is not available, use plain yogurt instead.

MAKES 12

2 cups self-rising flour
1 teaspoon baking soda
Scant $^2/_3$ cup superfine sugar
6 tablespoons vegetable oil
$^2/_3$ cup low-fat lemon-flavored yogurt
Finely grated zest and juice of
　$^1/_2$ lemon
2 eggs, lightly beaten
1 cup fresh raspberries

1. Preheat the oven to 375°F. Grease a 12-cup muffin pan or line the cups with paper muffin cups.

2. Mix the flour, baking soda, and sugar in a large bowl. In a separate bowl, mix together the vegetable oil, yogurt, lemon zest, and juice and eggs. Add the wet ingredients to the dry ingredients with the raspberries and mix briefly until just combined.

3. Spoon the batter into the prepared muffin cups, dividing it evenly. Bake in the oven for 15–18 minutes, or until risen and golden. Cool in the pan for 10 minutes, then turn out onto a wire rack. Serve warm or cold.

MUFFIN TIP
If you like, ice these muffins with a lemon glaze made from mixing together $^3/_4$ cup sifted powdered sugar and 1 tablespoon of lemon juice.

PEACH & BASIL Muffins

Use only the freshest peaches in season to get the best results. If you want to make these muffins out of season, use canned peaches in fruit juice, well-drained.

MAKES 12

2 ripe peaches, peeled, pitted, and
   chopped into small cubes
2 tablespoons chopped fresh basil
3 tablespoons light brown sugar
Grated zest and juice of $\frac{1}{2}$ lemon
2 cups self-rising flour
$\frac{1}{2}$ teaspoon baking powder
$\frac{1}{4}$ cup butter
Generous $\frac{1}{2}$ cup sugar
1 egg, lightly beaten
$\frac{2}{3}$ cup milk

1. Place the peaches in a bowl with the basil, brown sugar, and lemon juice and stir to mix. Set aside to stand for about 30 minutes.

2. Preheat the oven to 400°F. Grease a 12-cup muffin pan or line the cups with paper muffin cups.

3. Mix the flour and baking powder in a large bowl, then rub in the butter until the mixture resembles fine breadcrumbs. Stir in the sugar and lemon zest.

4. In a separate bowl, mix together the egg and milk. Add the wet ingredients to the dry ingredients alternately with the peaches and their juices, mixing briefly until just combined.

5. Spoon the mixture into the prepared muffin cups, dividing it evenly. Bake in the oven for about 20 minutes, or until risen and golden. Cool in the pan for 10 minutes, then turn out onto a wire rack. Serve warm or cold.

MUFFIN TIP
For a tasty alternative, use fresh nectarines in place of peaches, when they are in season.

BLUEBERRY Muffins

Someone once said that "When a man grows tired of blueberry muffins, he grows tired of life." You will never tire of these delicious fruity muffins!

MAKES 12

2 cups self-rising flour
1 teaspoon baking powder
1/4 cup butter
Generous 1/3 cup superfine sugar
1 cup fresh blueberries
2 eggs, lightly beaten
1 cup milk
1 teaspoon vanilla extract

1. Preheat the oven to 400°F. Grease a 12-cup muffin pan or line the cups with paper muffin cups.

2. Mix the flour and baking powder in a large bowl. Rub in the butter until the mixture resembles fine breadcrumbs. Stir the sugar and blueberries into this mixture.

3. In a separate small bowl, mix together the eggs, milk, and vanilla extract. Pour the egg mixture all at once into the dry ingredients and mix briefly until just combined.

4. Spoon the batter into the prepared muffin cups, dividing it evenly. Bake in the oven for about 20 minutes, or until risen and golden. Cool in the pan for 10 minutes, then turn out onto a wire rack. Serve warm or cold.

MUFFIN TIP
Try using fresh raspberries instead of blueberries, and replace the vanilla extract with 1 teaspoon ground pumpkin pie spice or ground cinnamon, if you like.

CHERRY COCONUT Muffins

Don't try using fresh cherries for this recipe—they will add too much moisture to the batter. These muffins are best made in a non-stick muffin pan, rather than with paper muffin cups.

MAKES 12

2 cups self-rising flour
¼ cup soft margarine
⅔ cup glacé cherries, chopped
1 cup flaked coconut
1 tablespoon superfine sugar
¼ teaspoon salt
2 eggs, lightly beaten
2 cup milk

1. Preheat the oven to 400°F. Grease a 12-cup non-stick muffin pan.

2. Put the flour in a bowl with the margarine, and blend with a fork until evenly mixed. Stir in the cherries, coconut, sugar and salt until well mixed.

3. In a separate bowl, mix together the eggs and milk. Add the egg mixture to the dry ingredients and mix briefly until just combined.

4. Spoon the batter into the prepared muffin cups, dividing it evenly. Bake in the oven for 15–20 minutes, or until risen and golden. Cool in the pan for 10 minutes, then turn out onto a wire rack. Serve warm or cold.

MUFFIN TIP
Chopped dried cherries or chopped dried apricots, used in place of the glacé cherries, would also work well in this recipe.

PLUM & MARZIPAN Muffins

The marzipan softens and melts a little during the baking of these muffins and tastes fabulous with the tart, fresh plums.

MAKES 12

1 cup all-purpose flour
1 cup whole-wheat flour
1 cup rolled oats
4 teaspoons baking powder
³/₄ teaspoon salt
1 cup wheat bran
³/₄ cup light brown sugar
1¹/₂ cups unpeeled pitted plums, chopped
³/₄ cup unsweetened orange juice
¹/₂ cup vegetable oil
2 eggs, lightly beaten
Finely grated zest of ¹/₂ orange
¹/₂ cup marzipan, cut into small cubes
¹/₄ cup flaked almonds

1. Preheat the oven to 350°F. Grease a 12-cup muffin pan or line the cups with paper muffin cups.

2. Mix the flours, oats, baking powder, salt, wheat bran, and sugar in a large bowl. In a separate bowl, mix together the plums, orange juice, vegetable oil, eggs, and orange zest.

3. Add the wet ingredients to the dry ingredients along with the marzipan and flaked almonds and mix briefly until just combined.

4. Spoon the batter into the prepared muffin cups, dividing it evenly. Bake in the oven for 25–30 minutes, or until risen and golden. Cool in the pan for 10 minutes, then turn out onto a wire rack. Serve warm or cold.

BANOFFEE Muffins

These moist banana muffins with their rich toffee-fudge sauce are absolutely delicious served warm. They are best made in a non-stick muffin pan, rather than with paper muffin cups.

MAKES 12

2 cups self-rising flour
½ teaspoon baking powder
1 teaspoon baking soda
½ teaspoon ground pumpkin pie spice
½ teaspoon salt
3 large well-ripened bananas, about 1lb unpeeled weight
½ cup superfine sugar
1 egg, lightly beaten
6 tablespoons milk
6 tablespoons butter, melted
1 teaspoon vanilla extract

FOR THE TOFFEE-FUDGE SAUCE
¼ cup butter
⅓ cup light brown sugar
¼ cup superfine sugar
1½ cups light corn syrup
½ cup heavy cream
1 tablespoon lemon juice
1 teaspoon vanilla extract

1. Preheat the oven to 375°F. Grease a 12-cup non-stick muffin pan.

2. For the muffins, mix the flour, baking powder, baking soda, pumpkin pie spice, and salt in a large bowl. In a separate bowl, mash the peeled bananas thoroughly with a potato masher or fork until puréed. Stir in the sugar, egg, milk, melted butter, and vanilla extract. Add the wet ingredients to the dry ingredients and mix briefly until just combined.

3. Spoon the batter into the prepared muffin cups, dividing it evenly. Bake in the oven for 18–20 minutes, or until well risen, golden and firm to the touch. Cool in the pan for 5 minutes, then turn out onto a wire rack.

4. For the toffee-fudge sauce, melt the butter, sugars, and corn syrup in a medium heavy-based saucepan over a very low heat. Cook gently, stirring frequently for 5 minutes. Remove the pan from the heat and slowly stir in the cream, lemon juice, and vanilla extract. Pour the sauce over the muffins and serve warm.

BLUEBERRY BUTTERMILK Muffins

If using frozen blueberries, thaw them thoroughly and pat dry on kitchen paper before tossing in powdered sugar.

MAKES 12

1 cup fresh or frozen blueberries
2 tablespoons powdered sugar
2 cups all-purpose flour
2 teaspoons baking powder
Pinch of salt
3/4 cup light brown sugar
1 egg, lightly beaten
1 cup buttermilk
2 tablespoons milk
1/4 cup butter, melted
Finely grated zest of 1/2 orange

1. Preheat the oven to 400°F. Grease a 12-cup muffin pan or line the cups with paper muffin cups.

2. Put the blueberries into a large bowl. Sift over the powdered sugar and toss the blueberries in the sugar to coat. Add the flour, baking powder, salt, and brown sugar, then stir together.

3. In a separate bowl, mix together the egg, buttermilk, milk, melted butter, and orange zest. Add the buttermilk mixture all at once to the dry ingredients and mix briefly until just combined.

4. Spoon the batter into the prepared muffin cups, dividing it evenly. Bake in the oven for 18–20 minutes, or until risen and golden. Cool in the pan for 5 minutes, then turn out onto a wire rack. Serve warm or cold.

MUFFIN TIP
Instead of butter, you can use 1/4 cup of sunflower oil, if you prefer.

APPLE STREUSEL Muffins

These moist muffins are studded with fresh chunks of apple and juicy golden raisins.
A grated streusel topping adds a lovely crunchy texture.

MAKES 12

1³/₄ cups all-purpose flour
2¹/₂ teaspoons baking powder
1¹/₂ teaspoons ground cinnamon
1 teaspoon ground ginger
Pinch of freshly grated nutmeg
¹/₂ teaspoon salt
²/₃ cup superfine sugar
1 egg, lightly beaten
²/₃ cup milk
6 tablespoons vegetable oil
¹/₃ cup golden raisins
3 medium apples (about 8 ounces
    whole/unprepared weight), peeled,
    cored and chopped

FOR THE TOPPING

¹/₃ cup all-purpose flour
3 tablespoons butter
2 tablespoons light brown sugar

1. Preheat the oven to 375°F. Grease a 12-cup muffin pan or line the cups with paper muffin cups.

2. For the topping, sift the flour into a bowl. Cut the butter into small pieces and rub into the flour until the mixture resembles fine breadcrumbs. Stir in the sugar, then gather the dough together and gently squeeze it into a ball. Coarsely grate the dough and set aside.

3. For the muffins, mix the flour, baking powder, cinnamon, ginger, nutmeg, salt, and sugar in a large bowl. In a separate bowl, mix together the egg, milk, vegetable oil, golden raisins, and chopped apples. Add the apple mixture all at once to the dry ingredients and mix briefly until just combined.

4. Spoon the batter into the prepared muffin cups, dividing it evenly, then sprinkle the tops with the grated topping. Bake in the oven for about 20 minutes, or until risen and golden. Cool in the pan for 10 minutes, then turn out onto a wire rack. Serve warm or cold.

MUFFIN TIP
If time allows, wrap and chill the streusel dough in the fridge for 15 minutes to make it easier to grate.

CLEMENTINE Muffins

If fresh clementines are not available, substitute a small (8 ounce) can of mandarin segments, well drained and chopped.

MAKES **12**

2 cups all-purpose flour
2 teaspoons baking powder
$\frac{1}{2}$ teaspoon salt
$\frac{1}{4}$ teaspoon ground allspice
$\frac{1}{4}$ teaspoon freshly grated nutmeg
Generous $\frac{1}{2}$ cup superfine sugar
$\frac{1}{3}$ cup margarine or butter
1 egg, lightly beaten
Scant 1 cup milk
3 clementines or mandarin oranges, peeled, broken into segments and chopped

FOR THE TOPPING (OPTIONAL)
Generous $\frac{1}{4}$ cup superfine sugar
$\frac{1}{2}$ teaspoon ground cinnamon
$\frac{1}{4}$ cup butter, melted

1. Preheat the oven to 350°F. Grease a 12-cup muffin pan or line the cups with paper muffin cups.

2. For the muffins, mix the flour, baking powder, salt, allspice, nutmeg, and sugar in a large bowl. Rub in the margarine or butter until the mixture resembles fine breadcrumbs.

3. In a separate bowl, mix together the egg and milk, then add the egg mixture all at once to the dry ingredients. Mix briefly until just combined, then fold in the clementine or mandarin pieces.

4. Spoon the batter into the prepared muffin cups, dividing it evenly. Bake in the oven for 20–25 minutes, or until risen and golden.

5. Meanwhile, for the topping, mix together the sugar and cinnamon in a small bowl and set aside. Remove the baked muffins from the pan while still warm. Dip the tops of the muffins in melted butter, then dip them in the cinnamon sugar. Transfer to a wire rack and allow to cool for 10 minutes before serving. Serve warm or cold.

SOUR CHERRY Muffins
filled with Jelly

If you don't have any fresh cherries, use canned or jarred pitted cherries for this recipe. Make sure they are well drained.

MAKES 12

2 cups all-purpose flour
1 teaspoon baking powder
$\frac{1}{2}$ teaspoon baking soda
$\frac{1}{2}$ teaspoon salt
$\frac{1}{2}$ teaspoon ground cardamom
Generous $\frac{1}{2}$ cup superfine sugar
1 cup fresh cherries, stoned and
  coarsely chopped
$\frac{1}{4}$ cup butter, melted
1 egg, lightly beaten
1 cup sour cream
$\frac{1}{2}$ teaspoon vanilla extract
3–4 tablespoons sour cherry jelly
3 tablespoons slivered almonds

1. Preheat the oven to 400°F. Grease a 12-cup muffin pan or line the cups with paper muffin cups.

2. Mix the flour, baking powder, baking soda, salt, and cardamom in a large bowl. Stir in the sugar and cherries and mix well.

3. In a separate bowl, beat together the melted butter, egg, sour cream, and vanilla extract. Pour the wet ingredients into the flour mixture and mix briefly until just combined.

4. Spoon half of the batter evenly into the prepared muffin cups. Add about 1 teaspoon of jelly to each, then top with the remaining batter, dividing it evenly. Sprinkle the tops with the flaked almonds.

5. Bake in the oven for about 20 minutes, or until risen and golden Cool in the pan for 10 minutes, then turn out onto a wire rack. Serve warm or cold.

TROPICAL FRUIT Muffins with Passion Fruit Glaze

Fresh mango, pineapple, and flaked coconut add delicious flavor to these passion fruit-glazed muffins.

MAKES 12

1 small, very ripe mango, peeled, and pitted
2 cups all-purpose flour
4 teaspoons baking powder
1/2 teaspoon salt
1 cup superfine sugar
1/2 cup flaked coconut
1/4 cup vegetable oil
1 cup milk
1 egg, lightly beaten
1 cup canned crushed pineapple in juice, drained

FOR THE PASSION FRUIT GLAZE
4 ripe passion fruit
4 tablespoons sugar

1. Preheat the oven to 400°F. Grease a 12-cup muffin pan or line the cups with paper muffin cups. Purée the mango flesh in a blender or food processor. Set aside.

2. Mix the flour, baking powder, salt, and superfine sugar in a large bowl. Stir in the coconut. In a separate bowl, mix together the vegetable oil, milk, and egg. Add the wet ingredients to the dry ingredients and mix briefly until just combined. Fold in the mango purée and drained pineapple.

3. Spoon the batter into the prepared muffin cups, dividing it evenly. Bake in the oven for 15–18 minutes, or until risen and golden.

4. Meanwhile, for the passion fruit glaze, cut each passion fruit in half and scoop out the flesh and juice, then press the pulp through a strainer into a small saucepan. Discard the seeds. Add the sugar to the pan and stir over a low heat until the sugar has dissolved. Increase the heat and bring the mixture to the boil, then boil for 3 minutes or until syrupy. Remove the pan from the heat.

5. Spoon the passion fruit syrup over the muffins while they are still hot. Allow them to cool slightly in the pan. Serve warm or just cooled.

CARROT, APPLE & COCONUT Muffins

This is an unusual combination that makes very moist muffins. Dried apple is readily available from health food stores and many large supermarkets.

MAKES 12

1 cup whole-wheat flour
1 cup all-purpose flour
$3/4$ cup superfine sugar
2 teaspoons baking powder
1 teaspoon ground cinnamon
$1/2$ teaspoon baking soda
1 cup carrot, finely grated
Scant 1 cup dried apple, chopped
$1/2$ cup raisins
$1/3$ cup walnuts, chopped
$1/2$ cup flaked coconut
2 eggs, lightly beaten
$1/2$ cup buttermilk
$1/2$ cup milk
2 teaspoons vanilla extract

1. Preheat the oven to 350°F. Grease a 12-cup muffin pan or line the cups with paper muffin cup.

2. Mix the flours, sugar, baking powder, cinnamon, and baking soda in a large bowl. Stir in the carrot, apple, raisins, walnuts, and coconut.

3. In a separate bowl, mix together the eggs, buttermilk, milk, and vanilla extract. Add the wet ingredients all at once to the dry ingredients and mix briefly until just combined. Carefully spoon the batter into the prepared muffin cups, dividing it evenly.

4. Bake in the oven for 20–25 minutes, or until risen and golden. Cool in the pan for 10 minutes, then turn out onto a wire rack. Serve warm or cold.

MUFFIN TIP
Try dried pear instead of apple in this recipe if you prefer.

PEACH UPSIDE-DOWN Muffins

These muffins are best made in a non-stick muffin pan, rather than with paper muffin cups.

MAKES 12

$^1/_3$ cup cold butter, cut into 12 pieces

$^1/_2$ cup light brown sugar

14-ounce can peach slices in fruit juice, drained

$1^1/_3$ cups all-purpose flour

1 cup superfine sugar

2 teaspoons baking powder

$^1/_2$ teaspoon salt

2 eggs, lightly beaten

$^2/_3$ cup sour cream

2 tablespoons margarine, melted

1. Preheat the oven to 375°F. Grease a 12-cup non-stick muffin pan.

2. Divide the butter and brown sugar evenly between the cups of the prepared pan. Place in the oven for about 5 minutes, or until the butter and sugar have melted. Remove from the oven and arrange the peach slices in the bottoms of the muffin cups.

3. Meanwhile, mix the flour, sugar, baking powder, and salt in a large bowl. In a separate bowl, mix together the eggs, sour cream, and melted margarine. Add the wet ingredients all at once to the dry ingredients and mix briefly until just combined.

4. Spoon the batter on top of the peach slices in the muffin cups, dividing it evenly. Bake in the oven for 20–25 minutes, or until risen and golden. Cool in the pan for about 10 minutes, then invert the muffins onto a plate or platter. Serve warm.

MUFFIN TIP
Use chopped canned pineapple, drained, in place of peach slices, if you prefer.

SOUR CREAM & GOLDEN RAISIN Muffins with Cinnamon Honey Butter

Briefly soaking the raisins in hot water makes them plump and juicy and ensures the muffins remain moist.

MAKES 12

1 cup golden raisins
1 cup boiling water
2$\frac{1}{2}$ cups self-rising flour
1 teaspoon baking powder
Scant 1 cup superfine sugar
Finely grated zest of 1 lemon
$\frac{3}{4}$ cup sour cream
$\frac{1}{2}$ cup milk
2 eggs, lightly beaten

FOR THE CINNAMON HONEY BUTTER
$\frac{1}{2}$ cup butter, softened
1 teaspoon ground cinnamon
1 tablespoon clear honey
$\frac{3}{4}$ cup powdered sugar, sifted

1. Preheat the oven to 375°F. Grease a 12-cup muffin pan or line the cups with paper muffin cups.

2. For the muffins, put the raisins in a bowl and pour over the boiling water. Leave to soak for 10 minutes, then drain well.

3. Meanwhile, mix the flour, baking powder, sugar, and lemon zest in a large bowl. In a separate bowl, mix together the sour cream, milk, eggs, and soaked raisins. Add the sour cream mixture to the dry ingredients, mixing briefly until just combined.

4. Spoon the batter into the prepared muffin cups, dividing it evenly. Bake in the oven for about 20 minutes, or until risen and golden. Cool in the pan for 5 minutes, then turn out onto a wire rack.

5. For the cinnamon honey butter, in a bowl, beat together the butter, cinnamon, and honey. Gradually beat in the powdered sugar until the mixture is pale and fluffy. Serve the muffins warm or cold with the butter.

PINEAPPLE & COCONUT Muffins

Like a piña colada without the rum, these muffins owe their moist texture to the combination of rich pineapple and coconut—a little delicious taste of the tropics in one bite!

MAKES 12

2 cups all-purpose flour
4 teaspoons baking powder
1/2 teaspoon salt
1 cup superfine sugar
3/4 cup fresh coconut flesh, grated
1/4 cup vegetable oil
1 cup milk
1 egg, lightly beaten
2/3 cup canned crushed pineapple in juice, drained

1. Preheat the oven to 400°F. Grease a 12-cup muffin pan or line the cups with paper muffin cups.

2. Mix the flour, baking powder, salt, and sugar in a large bowl. Stir in the coconut. In a separate bowl, mix together the vegetable oil, milk, and egg. Add the wet ingredients to the dry ingredients and mix briefly until just combined, then stir in the drained pineapple.

3. Spoon the batter into the prepared muffin cups, dividing it evenly. Bake in the oven for 15–18 minutes, or until risen and golden. Cool in the pan for 10 minutes, then turn out onto a wire rack. Serve warm or cold.

MUFFIN TIP
If you can't buy fresh coconut, use flaked or dried coconut instead.

LIME & FRESH COCONUT
Muffins

Fresh coconuts are not difficult to deal with, but you must drain the coconut water before cracking them open completely. Using a metal skewer, punch a hole in two of the three "eyes" at one end and drain the coconut water out. Bash the coconut as hard as you can with a hammer to open, then remove the flesh before grating.

MAKES 12

1$^{1}/_{2}$ cups fresh coconut flesh, grated
2 cups self-rising flour
1 cup superfine sugar
Finely grated zest and juice of 3 limes
1 egg, lightly beaten
1 cup milk
$^{1}/_{3}$ cup butter, melted

1. Preheat the oven to 400°F. Grease a 12-cup muffin pan or line the cups with paper muffin cups.

2. Set aside about 3 tablespoons of the coconut. Mix the flour and sugar in a large bowl. Add the remaining coconut and the lime zest and mix well.

3. In a separate bowl, mix together the lime juice, egg, milk, and melted butter. Add the wet ingredients to the dry ingredients and mix briefly until just combined.

4. Spoon the batter into the prepared muffin cups, dividing it evenly, then sprinkle the tops with the reserved coconut. Bake in the oven for about 20 minutes, or until risen and golden. Cool in the pan for 10 minutes, then turn out onto a wire rack. Serve warm or cold.

DRIED CHERRY, APPLE & PECAN Muffins

If dried cherries are not available, try making these delicious fruit and nut muffins with dried cranberries instead.

MAKES 12

2 cups all-purpose flour

1 cup superfine sugar

1 tablespoon baking powder

$^1/_2$ teaspoon salt

1 large apple, cored and coarsely chopped (leave skin on)

1 cup dried cherries, coarsely chopped

$^2/_3$ cup pecans, chopped

2 eggs, lightly beaten

$^1/_2$ cup butter, melted

$^3/_4$ cup buttermilk

3 tablespoons demerara sugar

1 teaspoon ground cinnamon

1. Preheat the oven to 400°F. Grease a 12-cup muffin pan or line the cups with paper muffin cups.

2. Mix the flour, superfine sugar, baking powder, and salt in a large bowl. Stir in the apple, cherries, and pecans.

3. In a separate bowl, mix together the eggs, melted butter, and buttermilk. Add the egg mixture all at once to the dry ingredients and mix briefly until just combined.

4. Spoon the batter into the prepared muffins cups, dividing it evenly. Combine the demerara sugar and cinnamon and sprinkle evenly over the muffins. Bake in the oven for about 20 minutes, or until risen and golden. Cool in the pan for 10 minutes, then turn out onto a wire rack. Serve warm or cold.

MUFFIN TIP

Try changing the nuts in this recipe for a different flavor. You could substitute almonds or walnuts for the pecans, for example.

STRAWBERRIES & CREAM
Muffins

These vanilla-flavored muffins are filled with strawberry conserve, and
topped with whipped cream and fresh strawberries.

MAKES 10

1³/₄ cups all-purpose flour
1 tablespoon baking powder
Pinch of salt
²/₃ cup superfine sugar
1 egg, lightly beaten
1 cup milk
7 tablespoons butter, melted
2 teaspoons vanilla extract
5–6 heaping tablespoons strawberry
   conserve
²/₃ cup whipping or heavy cream
2 teaspoons powdered sugar
Small or medium strawberries,
   halved, to decorate

1. Preheat the oven to 375°F. Grease 10 cups of a 12-cup non-stick muffin pan.

2. Mix the flour, baking powder, salt, and superfine sugar in a large bowl. In a separate bowl or jug, mix together the egg, milk, melted butter and vanilla extract. Add the milk mixture all at once to the dry ingredients and mix briefly until just combined.

3. Spoon the batter into the prepared muffin cups, dividing it evenly. Bake in the oven for about 20 minutes, or until risen and golden. Cool in the pan for 10 minutes, then turn out onto a wire rack and leave to cool completely.

4. When the muffins are cold, cut each one in half horizontally. Spread strawberry conserve on the bottom half of each muffin and replace the top half.

5. Whip the cream with the powdered sugar in a small bowl until soft peaks form. Either spoon or pipe a swirl of cream on top of each muffin. Arrange the strawberry halves on top of the muffins. Chill until ready to serve.

LEMON POPPY SEED
Muffins

It's best to make these muffins in a non-stick muffin pan without paper
muffin cups so that the syrup can soak into the muffins without
running under the paper.

MAKES 12

Finely grated zest and juice
   of 2 lemons
1 cup superfine sugar
2 cups self-rising flour
2 tablespoons poppy seeds
1 egg, lightly beaten
1 milk milk
$^{1}/_{3}$ cup butter, melted

FOR THE LEMON SYRUP
$^{3}/_{4}$ cup powdered sugar, sifted
Juice of 1 lemon

1. Preheat the oven to 400°F. Grease a 12-cup non-stick muffin pan.

2. For the muffins, mix 2 teaspoons of the lemon zest and 2 tablespoons
of the sugar in a small bowl. Set aside.

3. Mix the flour, poppy seeds, and remaining sugar in a large bowl. In a
separate bowl, mix together the remaining lemon zest, the lemon juice,
egg, milk, and melted butter. Add this to the flour and sugar mixture and
stir until just combined.

4. Spoon the batter into the prepared muffin cups, dividing it evenly,
then sprinkle the tops with the reserved sugar and lemon zest mixture.
Bake in the oven for about 20 minutes, or until risen and golden.

5. Meanwhile, for the lemon syrup, mix the powdered sugar and lemon
juice in a bowl until smooth and well blended. Spoon the lemon syrup
over the hot baked muffins, then let them cool in the pan. Turn out
and serve cold.

PINEAPPLE & PASSION FRUIT Muffins

MAKES **10**

4 ripe passion fruit

8-ounce can crushed pineapple in fruit juice

About 5 tablespoons unsweetened pineapple or orange juice

2 cups self-rising flour

1 teaspoon baking powder

$\frac{1}{4}$ teaspoon baking soda

$\frac{1}{4}$ teaspoon salt

$\frac{1}{2}$ cup superfine sugar

1 egg, lightly beaten

6 tablespoons vegetable oil

FOR THE PASSION FRUIT TOPPING

$\frac{1}{4}$ cup butter, softened

$\frac{3}{4}$ cup powdered sugar, sifted

Toasted coconut flakes, for sprinkling

MUFFIN TIP
Make sure that the passion fruit are really ripe before extracting the juice; their skins should be very wrinkly and dimpled.

1. Preheat the oven to 375°F. Grease 10 cups of a 12-cup muffin pan or line 10 cups with paper muffin cups.

2. For the muffins, halve the passion fruit and scoop out the flesh and juice into a fine strainer placed over a bowl. Press the pulp with the back of a spoon to squeeze out all the juice. Discard the seeds. Reserve 1 tablespoon of the juice for the icing. Pour the pineapple into the strainer and press out most of the juice. Measure the juice in the bowl and make up to 1 cup with the pineapple or orange juice. Set aside.

3. Mix the flour, baking powder, baking soda, salt, and sugar in a large bowl. Stir the egg, vegetable oil, and crushed pineapple into the fruit juice in the bowl. Add the pineapple mixture all at once to the dry ingredients and mix briefly until just combined.

4. Spoon the batter into the prepared muffin cups, dividing evenly. Bake in the oven for about 20 minutes, or until risen and golden. Cool in the pan for 10 minutes, then turn onto a wire rack and leave to cool completely.

5. For the passion fruit topping, beat the butter in a bowl until creamy. Gradually beat in two-thirds of the powdered sugar. Beat in the reserved passion fruit juice, then add the rest of the powdered sugar, beating until the mixture is light and fluffy. Spread a little of the topping mixture over the top of each muffin and sprinkle with toasted coconut flakes to serve.

BUTTERY APPLE CUSTARD Muffins

Here the apples are gently cooked in butter until tender, then tossed in ground cinnamon. A small amount of custard powder lightens the mixture and gives it a subtle golden color.

MAKES 12

$\frac{1}{2}$ cup butter, melted

2 apples, peeled, cored, and finely chopped

$1\frac{1}{2}$ teaspoons ground cinnamon

$1\frac{3}{4}$ cups all-purpose flour

$\frac{1}{4}$ cup custard powder

1 cup superfine sugar

1 tablespoon baking powder

$\frac{1}{2}$ teaspoon salt

2 eggs, lightly beaten

$\frac{3}{4}$ cup buttermilk

2 tablespoons demerara sugar

MUFFIN TIP
If you don't have any custard powder, use cornstarch instead. It will give the same light texture, but won't add any color to the muffins.

1. Preheat the oven to 400°F. Grease a 12-cup muffin pan or line the cups with paper muffin cups.

2. Pour about half of the melted butter into a heavy-based non-stick saucepan. Add the apples and cook gently for 10 minutes, or until very tender. Sprinkle over the cinnamon and stir in. Remove the pan from the heat and set aside to cool for 5 minutes.

3. Mix the flour, custard powder, superfine sugar, baking powder, and salt in a large bowl. In a separate bowl, mix together the eggs, buttermilk, remaining melted butter, and apple mixture. Add the wet ingredients to the dry ingredients, and mix briefly until just combined.

4. Spoon the batter into the prepared muffin cups, dividing it evenly. Sprinkle the demerara sugar evenly over the tops of the muffins. Bake in the oven for about 20 minutes, or until risen and golden. Cool in the pan for 10 minutes, then turn out onto a wire rack. Serve warm or cold.

SUGAR-CRUSTED CITRUS Muffins

These light lemon and lime muffins have a tangy topping that separates into a sticky syrup and a crunchy sugary crust.

MAKES 10

1³/₄ cups self-rising flour
1 teaspoon baking powder
¹/₂ teaspoon salt
¹/₂ cup superfine sugar
1 cup milk
Finely grated zest of ¹/₂ lemon
Finely grated zest of ¹/₂ lime
1 egg, lightly beaten
6 tablespoons butter, melted

FOR THE CRUNCHY TOPPING
¹/₂ cup sugar
Juice of 1 small lemon
Thinly pared strips of rind of ¹/₂ lemon
Thinly pared strips of rind of ¹/₂ lime

1. Preheat the oven to 375°F. Grease 10 cups of a 12-cup muffin pan or line 10 cups with paper muffin cups.

2. For the muffins, mix the flour, baking powder, salt and sugar in a large bowl. Pour the milk into a bowl. Stir in the lemon and lime zest, egg and melted butter. Add the wet ingredients to the dry ingredients and mix briefly until just combined.

3. Spoon the batter into the prepared muffin cups, dividing it evenly. Bake in the oven for about 20 minutes, or until risen and golden. Remove from the oven and leave the baked muffins in the pan.

4. While the muffins are baking, make the crunchy topping. Mix the sugar and lemon juice in a bowl until blended. Stir in the thinly pared strips of lemon and lime rind. When the muffins come out of the oven, spoon the citrus mixture over the hot muffins. Leave to cool in the pan, then turn out and serve.

MUFFIN TIP
Make sure you use granulated and not superfine sugar for the topping.

JELLY-FILLED MINI Muffins

You can use this recipe to make 12 regular-sized muffins
if you prefer a larger treat.

MAKES 36

1²/₃ cups self-rising flour
1 teaspoon baking powder
¹/₄ cup butter
¹/₃ cup superfine sugar
2 eggs, lightly beaten
1 cup milk
1 teaspoon vanilla extract
5–6 tablespoons raspberry or
strawberry jelly

FOR THE TOPPING
¹/₄ cup butter
1 teaspoon ground cinnamon
¹/₄ cup sugar

1. Preheat the oven to 400°F. Grease three 12-cup mini muffin pans or
one 24-cup mini muffin pan and one 12-cup mini muffin pan, or line the
cups with paper mini muffin cups.

2. For the muffins, mix the flour and baking powder in a large bowl. Rub in
the butter until the mixture resembles fine breadcrumbs. Stir in the sugar.

3. In a separate small bowl, mix together the eggs, milk, and vanilla
extract, then pour the milk mixture all at once into the dry ingredients
and mix briefly until just combined.

4. Put a small spoonful of the mixture into each prepared muffin cup.
Add about ¹/₂ teaspoon of jelly to each, then top with the remaining
muffin batter, dividing it evenly. Bake in the oven for 8–10 minutes, or
until well risen, golden and firm to the touch. Cool in the pan for a few
minutes, then turn out onto a wire rack.

5. For the topping, melt the butter in a small saucepan over a low heat,
then remove the pan from the heat. In a small bowl, mix together the
cinnamon and sugar. Brush each baked warm mini muffin all over with a
little melted butter, then roll in the cinnamon sugar. Set aside to cool.
Serve warm or cold.

CHRISTMAS Muffins

Incredibly quick and simple to make, these are great during the festive period.

MAKES 10

2 cups self-rising flour
1 teaspoon baking powder
1 teaspoon ground pumpkin pie spice
1/2 cup light brown sugar
1 cup fruit mincemeat
1 egg, lightly beaten
1/2 cup butter, melted
3/4 cup buttermilk
1 tablespoon milk
2 teaspoons demerara sugar

1. Preheat the oven to 400°F. Grease 10 cups of a 12-cup muffin pan or line 10 cups with paper muffin cups.

2. Mix the flour, baking powder, pumpkin pie spice, and brown sugar in a large bowl. In a separate bowl, mix together the mincemeat, egg, melted butter, buttermilk, and milk. Add the wet ingredients to the dry ingredients and mix briefly until just combined.

3. Spoon the batter into the prepared muffin cups, dividing it evenly, then sprinkle the tops with demerara sugar. Bake in the oven for 18–20 minutes, or until risen and golden. Cool in the pan for 10 minutes, then turn out onto a wire rack. Serve warm or cold.

MUFFIN TIP
Mincemeat (or fruit mince) contains dried fruit; spices such as cinnamon or nutmeg; nuts such as walnuts or chopped almonds; suet; and some kind of alcohol, usually either brandy or rum.

RED, WHITE & BLUE Muffins

Don't overdo the red and blue icing on these muffins; a subtle finish looks much more tempting.

MUFFIN TIP
If preferred, drizzle melted white chocolate on top of the muffins and sprinkle with chopped dried blueberries and cherries.

MAKES 12

2 cups all-purpose flour
2½ teaspoons baking powder
Generous ½ cup superfine sugar
½ teaspoon salt
½ cup dried cherries
½ cup dried blueberries
⅔ cup macadamia nuts, roughly
   chopped
1 cup milk
½ cup vegetable oil
1 egg, lightly beaten

FOR THE ICING

¾ cup powdered sugar
1 tablespoon warm water
Red and blue food coloring

1. Preheat the oven to 375°F. Grease a 12-cup muffin pan or line the cups with paper muffin cups.

2. For the muffins, mix the flour, baking powder, sugar, salt, dried cherries and blueberries, and macadamia nuts in a large bowl. In a separate bowl, mix together the milk, vegetable oil, and egg. Add the wet ingredients to the dry ingredients, mixing briefly until just combined.

3. Spoon the batter into the prepared muffin cups, dividing it evenly. Bake in the oven for about 18–20 minutes, or until risen and golden. Cool in the pan for 5 minutes, then turn onto a wire rack and leave to cool completely.

4. For the icing, sift the powdered sugar into a bowl and gradually blend in the water until you have a smooth icing. Color about a quarter of the icing red and a quarter blue, leaving half the icing white. Spread the white icing on top of all the muffins and leave to set. Fill two small piping bags with the red and blue icing, and drizzle stripes and spots over the white iced muffins. Leave the icing to set before serving.

CLEMENTINE & CRANBERRY Muffins

MAKES 12

3 small clementines, about 5 ounces
   in total weight
$^3/_4$ cup water
2 cups all-purpose flour
1$^1/_2$ teaspoons baking powder
$^1/_2$ teaspoon baking soda
Generous $^1/_2$ cup superfine sugar
$^1/_2$ teaspoon salt
1 cup dried cranberries
1 egg, lightly beaten
7 tablespoons butter, melted

FOR THE TOPPING
$^1/_2$ cup rolled oats
$^1/_4$ cup light brown sugar
2 heaping tablespoons all-purpose
   flour
1 teaspoon ground cinnamon
$^1/_4$ cup butter, cut into small pieces

1. Roughly chop the clementines (leaving their peel on), remove any seeds, then put the clementines in a small saucepan with the water. Bring to a boil, then reduce the heat, half-cover the pan with a lid, and simmer for 20 minutes, until really tender. Remove the pan from the heat and leave to cool for 10 minutes, then purée the mixture in a blender or food processor until smooth. Set aside.

2. Preheat the oven to 375°F. Grease a 12-cup muffin pan or line the cups with paper muffin cups.

3. Make the topping by placing all the ingredients in a bowl and rubbing in the butter. Alternatively, put all the ingredients in a food processor and process until lumps form. Set aside.

4. For the muffins, mix the flour, baking powder, baking soda, sugar, salt, and cranberries in a large bowl. Measure the clementine purée in a bowl and make up to 1 cup with water if needed. Stir in the egg and melted butter. Add to the dry ingredients and mix briefly until just combined.

5. Spoon the batter into the prepared muffin cups, dividing it evenly, then sprinkle the topping mixture evenly over the tops of the muffins. Bake in the oven for 18–20 minutes, or until well risen and golden. Cool in the pan for 5 minutes, then turn out onto a wire rack. Serve warm or cold.

MINI CONFETTI
Muffins

Decorate these tiny muffins with a selection of pretty icings in
the color theme of a wedding or baby shower.

MAKES 24

1 cup self-rising flour
1/2 teaspoon baking powder
1/4 cup superfine sugar
1/4 cup mixed candied fruit, very
    finely chopped
3 tablespoons vegetable oil
Finely grated zest of 1/2 small orange
1 tablespoon unsweetened
    orange juice
5 tablespoons low-fat plain yogurt
1 egg, lightly beaten

FOR THE ICING

3/4 cup powdered sugar
1 tablespoon warm water
A few drops of several different food
    colorings of your choice
Confetti-type sprinkles, to decorate

1. Preheat the oven to 375°F. Grease two 12-cup mini muffin pans or
one 24-cup mini muffin pan, or line the cups with paper mini muffin cups.

2. For the muffins, mix the flour, baking powder, sugar, and candied fruit
in a medium bowl. In a separate bowl, mix together the vegetable oil,
orange zest, orange juice, yogurt, and egg. Add the wet ingredients to the
dry ingredients and mix briefly until just combined.

3. Spoon the batter into the prepared muffin cups, dividing it evenly.
Bake in the oven for 10–12 minutes, or until well risen and firm to the
touch. Cool in the pans for 5 minutes, then turn out onto a wire rack and
leave to cool completely.

4. For the icing, sift the powdered sugar into a mixing bowl, add the
water, and blend until smooth. Divide the icing into two or three small
bowls and add a drop or two of food coloring to each to achieve the
desired colors. Mix well, then spoon a little icing on top of each mini
muffin, and decorate with a few sprinkles. Leave to set before serving.

EASTER Muffins

MAKES 10

1 cup self-rising flour
1/2 teaspoon baking soda
1/3 cup superfine sugar
1/4 cup butter, melted
5 tablespoons low-fat lemon-flavored yogurt
Finely grated zest of 1/2 lemon
1 tablespoon lemon juice
1 egg, lightly beaten

FOR THE LIME SYRUP
Finely grated zest and juice of 1 lime
2 heaping tablespoons superfine sugar

FOR THE ICING
1 1/2 cups powdered sugar
2 tablespoons butter, melted
3 tablespoons lemon juice
Yellow and green food coloring
30 mini sugar-coated Easter eggs

1. Preheat the oven to 375°F. Line 10 cups of a 12-cup muffin pan with paper muffin cups.

2. For the muffins, mix the flour, baking soda, and sugar in a large bowl. In a separate bowl, mix together the melted butter, yogurt, lemon zest, lemon juice, and egg. Add the wet ingredients to the dry ingredients and mix briefly until just combined.

3. Spoon the batter into the prepared muffin cups, dividing it evenly. Bake in the oven for about 15 minutes, or until risen and golden.

4. While the muffins are baking, make the lime syrup. Gently heat the lime zest and juice and sugar in a small saucepan until the sugar has dissolved. Remove the pan from the heat and leave to cool for 5 minutes, then pour the syrup through a fine strainer into a bowl. Drizzle a little of the warm syrup over each hot baked muffin. Leave to cool completely in the pan.

5. For the icing, sift the powdered sugar into a mixing bowl. Gently heat the butter and lemon juice in a small saucepan until melted. Pour the melted mixture over the powdered sugar and stir until smooth and glossy.

6. Spoon half of the icing into a separate bowl. Add two drops of yellow coloring to one icing and a drop of green coloring to the other. Stir until blended, then use the icings to decorate five of the cold muffins pale yellow and five pale green. Decorate each muffin with a cluster of three mini Easter eggs. Leave to set before serving.

NUT & SPICE
MUFFINS

MOIST ALMOND & PEAR Muffins

Pears and almonds have a natural affinity, as shown in these delectable muffins.

MAKES 12

2 cups all-purpose flour

1 tablespoon baking powder

$\frac{1}{4}$ teaspoon freshly grated nutmeg

4 tablespoons ground almonds

$\frac{2}{3}$ cup blanched almonds, chopped

$\frac{1}{2}$ cup marzipan, chopped into
  small pieces

$\frac{3}{4}$ cup light brown sugar

1 egg, lightly beaten

Scant 1 cup unsweetened pear or
  apple juice

6 tablespoons butter, melted

2 small ripe pears, peeled, cored,
  and chopped

$\frac{1}{4}$ cup flaked almonds

1 teaspoon powdered sugar

1. Preheat the oven to 375°F. Grease a 12-cup muffin pan or line the cups with paper muffin cups.

2. Mix the flour, baking powder, nutmeg, ground and chopped almonds, marzipan, and brown sugar in a large bowl. In a separate bowl, mix together the egg, pear or apple juice, melted butter, and pears. Add the pear mixture all at once to the dry ingredients and mix briefly until just combined.

3. Spoon the batter into the prepared muffin cups, dividing it evenly, then sprinkle the tops with flaked almonds. Bake in the oven for 18-20 minutes, or until well risen and golden.

4. Cool in the pan for 5 minutes, then turn out onto a wire rack. Dust the tops with sifted powdered sugar and serve warm or cold.

MUFFIN TIP
If available, use toasted blanched almonds for a more distinctive nutty flavor.

CARAMEL ORANGE
Muffins

MAKES 12

1 large orange, peeled
Generous $^1/_2$ cup sugar
2 tablespoons water
2$^1/_4$ cups self-rising flour
1 teaspoon baking powder
$^1/_2$ teaspoon ground cinnamon
$^1/_4$ teaspoon ground cloves
$^1/_4$ teaspoon ground allspice
Pinch of salt
$^1/_4$ cup butter
$^1/_3$ cup superfine sugar
$^1/_2$ cup pistachio nuts, chopped
2 eggs, lightly beaten
1 cup milk

1. Preheat the oven to 400°F. Grease a 12-cup muffin pan or line the cups with paper muffin cups.

2. Working over a bowl to collect any juice, cut the orange into segments, then coarsely chop them and add to the bowl. Set aside.

3. Combine the granulated sugar and water in a small, heavy-based saucepan and stir over a low heat until the sugar has dissolved. Increase the heat and bring the sugar mixture to a boil. Boil for about 7–10 minutes, or until the mixture has turned a dark caramel color.

4. Remove the pan from the heat, and carefully add the chopped orange flesh and all its juice. Be careful: the mixture will bubble fiercely. Allow the mixture to cool, then drain the oranges, reserving $^3/_4$ cup of the syrup.

5. Mix the flour, baking powder, cinnamon, cloves, allspice, and salt in a large bowl. Rub in the butter until the mixture resembles fine breadcrumbs, then stir in the superfine sugar and pistachio nuts, mixing well.

6. In a separate small bowl, mix together the eggs and milk, then pour into the dry ingredients. Add the drained oranges and mix until just combined. Spoon the batter into the muffin cups, dividing it evenly.

7. Bake in the oven for 18–20 minutes, or until well risen, golden, and firm to the touch. Spoon the reserved orange caramel syrup over the hot muffins. Cool in the pan for 10 minutes, then turn out onto a wire rack.

SPICED CARROT
Muffins

These muffins are really mini carrot cakes—perfect for lunchboxes and afternoon tea.

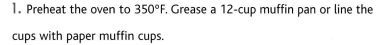

MAKES **12**

2 cups all-purpose flour
1 cup superfine sugar
2 teaspoons baking soda
2 teaspoons ground cinnamon
1 teaspoon salt
³/₄ cup vegetable oil
³/₄ cup milk
3 eggs, lightly beaten
¹/₂ cup peeled carrot, grated
1 cup walnuts, chopped
1 cup raisins

FOR THE FROSTING
Generous ¹/₃ cup cream cheese, softened
3 tablespoons butter, softened
1 cup powdered sugar, sifted
¹/₂ teaspoon vanilla extract

1. Preheat the oven to 350°F. Grease a 12-cup muffin pan or line the cups with paper muffin cups.

2. For the muffins, mix the flour, sugar, baking soda, cinnamon, and salt in a large bowl. In a separate bowl, mix together the vegetable oil, milk, and eggs. Add the wet ingredients all at once to the dry ingredients together with the grated carrot, walnuts and raisins. Mix briefly until just combined.

3. Spoon the batter into the muffin cups, dividing it evenly. Bake in the oven for 20–25 minutes, or until risen and golden. Cool in the pan for 10 minutes, then turn out onto a wire rack and leave to cool completely.

4. For the frosting, beat together the cream cheese and butter in a bowl until light and fluffy. Beat in the powdered sugar and vanilla extract until the topping is thick and spreadable. Spread a large tablespoonful of the topping mixture on top of each muffin before serving.

BANANA & HAZELNUT Muffins

To toast hazelnuts, or any other nuts for that matter, spread them in a single layer on a baking sheet and put into a fairly hot oven (about 400°F) for about 5 minutes, or until golden and fragrant (smaller nuts may take less time, while larger nuts may need a couple of minutes extra).

MAKES **12**

2 cups self-rising flour
2 tablespoons light brown sugar
1/3 cup toasted hazelnuts, chopped
3 large very ripe bananas, peeled
3 tablespoons vegetable oil
2 eggs, lightly beaten
1/3 cup plain yogurt
2 tablespoons demerara sugar

1. Preheat the oven to 400°F. Grease a 12-cup muffin pan or line the cups with paper muffin cups.

2. Mix the flour, brown sugar, and hazelnuts in a large bowl. In a separate bowl, mash the bananas until fairly smooth, then stir in the vegetable oil, eggs, and yogurt. Add the wet ingredients all at once to the dry ingredients and mix briefly until just combined.

3. Spoon the batter into the prepared muffin cups, dividing it evenly, then sprinkle the tops with the demerara sugar.

4. Bake in the oven for about 20 minutes, or until risen and golden. Cool in the pan for 10 minutes, then turn out onto a wire rack. Serve warm or cold.

MUFFIN TIP
Pecans, walnuts, or toasted almonds would also work well in this recipe instead of hazelnuts.

PEANUT BUTTER & BANANA Muffins

The combination of peanut butter and banana is a popular sandwich filling, used here to create these delicious muffins!

MAKES 12

1½ cups all-purpose flour
1 cup rolled oats
¼ cup light brown sugar
1 tablespoon baking powder
½ teaspoon salt
⅓ cup crunchy peanut butter
1 cup milk
1 tablespoon maple syrup
1 egg, lightly beaten
2 very ripe bananas, peeled and
   mashed
1 tablespoon sugar
1 teaspoon ground cinnamon

1. Preheat the oven to 400°F. Grease a 12-cup muffin pan or line the cups with paper muffin cups.

2. Mix the flour and oats in a large bowl, then stir in the brown sugar. Add the baking powder and salt, and stir to mix.

3. In a separate bowl, mix together the peanut butter, milk, maple syrup, egg, and mashed bananas until well blended. Add the wet ingredients all at once to the dry ingredients, mixing until just combined.

4. Spoon the batter into the prepared muffin cups, dividing it evenly. Mix together the sugar and cinnamon, then sprinkle this mixture over the tops of the muffins. Bake in the oven for about 20 minutes, or until risen and golden. Cool in the pan for 10 minutes, then turn out onto a wire rack. Serve warm or cold.

CINNAMON SWIRL
Muffins

Nothing could be more enticing than to break open these warm
fragrant muffins and discover ripples of cinnamon sugar.

MAKES 10

1³/₄ cups self-rising flour
1 teaspoon baking powder
Pinch of salt
¹/₂ cup superfine sugar
1 egg, lightly beaten
1 cup milk
7 tablespoons butter, melted

FOR THE CINNAMON SUGAR
2 teaspoons ground cinnamon
6 tablespoons light brown sugar

1. Preheat the oven to 375°F. Grease 10 cups of a 12-cup muffin pan or line 10 cups with paper muffin cups. For the cinnamon sugar, mix together the cinnamon and sugar in a small bowl. Set aside.

2. For the muffins, mix the flour, baking powder, salt, and sugar in a large bowl. In a separate bowl, mix together the egg, milk, and melted butter. Add the wet ingredients all at once to the dry ingredients and mix briefly until just combined.

3. Put a tablespoonful of batter into each prepared muffin cup. Sprinkle each muffin with a heaping teaspoon of cinnamon sugar, then spoon some more batter and cinnamon sugar into the muffin cups. Finish with a layer of batter, dividing it evenly. Using a fine skewer or the tip of a sharp knife, swirl the mixture in each muffin cup to achieve a marbled effect.

4. Bake in the oven for 18–20 minutes, or until risen and golden. Cool in the pan for 10 minutes (the sugar mixture will remain really hot, so don't be tempted to try them sooner), then turn out onto a wire rack. Serve warm or cold.

CARDAMOM & ORANGE Muffins

Cardamom is a delightful warm aromatic spice that has a natural affinity with oranges. These muffins are sprinkled with amber sugar crystals, which add a caramel flavor and crunchy texture to the muffins.

MAKES 12

4 green cardamom pods
2 cups self-rising flour
1 teaspoon baking powder
²/₃ cup superfine sugar
1 egg, lightly beaten
1 cup milk
Finely grated zest and juice of 1 large orange
6 tablespoons butter, melted
2 tablespoons demerara sugar

1. Preheat the oven to 375°F. Grease a 12-cup muffin pan or line the cups with paper muffin cups.

2. Split open the cardamom pods and use a mortar and pestle to crush the black seeds from the cardamom pods into a powder. Using a fine strainer, sift them with the flour and baking powder into a large bowl, discarding any large bits of spice left in the strainer. Stir in the superfine sugar.

3. In a separate bowl, mix together the egg, milk, orange zest and juice, and melted butter. Add the wet ingredients all at once to the dry ingredients and mix briefly until just combined.

4. Spoon the batter into the prepared muffin cups, dividing it evenly, then sprinkle the tops with demerara sugar. Bake in the oven for about 20 minutes, or until risen and firm to the touch. Cool in the pan for 5 minutes, then turn out onto a wire rack. Serve warm or cold.

MUFFIN TIP
If you prefer, use roughly crushed brown sugar cubes instead of demerara sugar for the topping of these muffins.

SWEET POTATO Muffins with Pecans & Cinnamon

The flavor of the sweet potato goes beautifully with the cinnamon, and the chopped pecans add a welcome crunch to these tasty muffins.

MAKES 12

1 large orange-fleshed sweet potato
1/2 cup butter, softened
1 cup superfine sugar
2 eggs, lightly beaten
2 cups all-purpose flour
2 teaspoons baking powder
1/4 teaspoon salt
1 teaspoon ground cinnamon
1/2 teaspoon freshly grated nutmeg
1 cup milk
1/2 cup pecans, chopped

MUFFIN TIP
Walnuts would also work well in this recipe instead of pecans, if you like.

1. Preheat the oven to 400°F. Grease a 12-cup muffin pan or line the cups with paper muffin cups.

2. Prick the sweet potato several times with a fork and place it on a small baking sheet or a piece of foil. Bake in the oven for 45–60 minutes, or until tender. Remove from the oven and set aside until cool enough to handle.

3. When cool, cut the sweet potato in half and scoop out the flesh. Transfer the flesh to a small bowl and mash until smooth—you should have about 1 cup mashed potato. Set aside.

4. Cream the butter and sugar together in a large bowl. Beat in the eggs and sweet potato. In a separate bowl, mix together the flour, baking powder, salt, cinnamon, and nutmeg. Add the flour mixture to the butter mixture alternately with the milk, mixing briefly until just combined. Fold in the pecans.

5. Spoon the batter into the prepared muffin cups, dividing it evenly. Bake in the oven for 20–25 minutes, or until risen and golden. Cool in the pan for 10 minutes, then turn out onto a wire rack. Serve warm or cold.

HONEY & PISTACHIO
Muffins

This recipe is inspired by baklava, the sweet and sticky Middle Eastern pastry flavored with nuts and honey. Use a scented honey for the best results.

MAKES 12

2 cups all-purpose flour
1 tablespoon baking powder
1/2 teaspoon salt
1 teaspoon ground cinnamon
Pinch of ground cloves
3 tablespoons chopped pistachio nuts
3 tablespoons chopped blanched
 almonds
1/2 cup light brown sugar
4 tablespoons clear honey
1 cup milk
2 tablespoons vegetable oil
2 eggs, lightly beaten

1. Preheat the oven to 400°F. Grease a 12-cup muffin pan or line the cups with paper muffin cups.

2. Mix the flour, baking powder, salt, cinnamon, and cloves in a large bowl. Stir in 2 tablespoons of the pistachio nuts, 2 tablespoons of the almonds, and the sugar.

3. In a separate bowl, mix together 2 tablespoons of the honey with the milk, vegetable oil, and eggs. Add the wet ingredients all at once to the dry ingredients and mix briefly until just combined.

4. Spoon the batter into the prepared muffin cups, dividing it evenly, then sprinkle the tops with the remaining mixed chopped nuts.

5. Bake in the oven for 18–20 minutes, or until risen and golden. Drizzle the hot baked muffins with the remaining 2 tablespoons of honey. Cool in the pan for 10 minutes, then turn out onto a wire rack. These muffins are best eaten warm.

COFFEE WALNUT Muffins

MAKES 12

²/₃ cup walnut halves
Scant ³/₄ cup butter
²/₃ cup sugar
3 egg whites
4 egg yolks
1 teaspoon vanilla extract
1 cup all-purpose flour
1 teaspoon baking powder

FOR THE COFFEE FROSTING
1¹/₂ tablespoons milk
Small pat of butter
1 tablespoon instant coffee granules
1¹/₂ cups powdered sugar, sifted
1 teaspoon vanilla extract

1. Preheat the oven to 350°F. Grease a 12-cup muffin pan or line the cups with paper muffin cups.

2. Reserve 12 walnut halves for decoration, then finely chop the remainder in a blender or food processor, but do not allow them to become pasty.

3. Melt the butter and sugar in a heavy-based saucepan over a low heat. Gently bring the mixture to a boil and cook for 2 minutes, stirring constantly. Be careful not to brown or burn the mixture. Remove the pan from the heat and set aside to cool.

4. Whisk the egg whites in a clean bowl until stiff peaks form; set aside. Add the egg yolks to the cooled sugar-butter mixture, then stir in the chopped walnuts, vanilla extract, flour, and baking powder. Gently fold in the whisked egg whites to make a soft, thick batter.

5. Spoon the batter into the prepared muffin cups, dividing evenly. Bake in the oven for 15–20 minutes, or until golden and firm to the touch. Cool in the pan for 10 minutes, then turn onto a wire rack to cool completely.

6. For the frosting, heat the milk, butter, and coffee granules in a small saucepan over a low heat, stirring until the butter is melted. Add the powdered sugar and vanilla extract and stir until smooth and combined, adding a little more powdered sugar if necessary to make a spreadable consistency. Spread some frosting on top of each muffin and decorate with a walnut half.

GINGER RHUBARB Muffins with Crème Anglaise

MAKES **10**

2 cups self-rising flour

2 teaspoons ground ginger

$1/2$ teaspoon baking powder

$1/2$ teaspoon baking soda

$1/4$ teaspoon salt

Scant $2/3$ cup superfine sugar

1 cup fresh rhubarb, finely chopped

1 egg, lightly beaten

$2/3$ cup milk

$2/3$ cup sour cream

4 tablespoons vegetable oil

1 tablespoon demerara sugar

FOR THE CRÈME ANGLAISE

$1^{1}/4$ cups milk

1 vanilla bean, split lengthwise

3 egg yolks

1 teaspoon cornstarch

1 tablespoon superfine sugar

1. Preheat the oven to 375°F. Grease 10 cups of a 12-cup muffin pan or line 10 cups with paper muffin cups. Start making the Crème Anglaise. Pour the milk into a heavy-based saucepan, add the vanilla bean and bring to a boil. Turn off the heat and leave to infuse for 15 minutes.

2. For the muffins, mix the flour, ginger, baking powder, baking soda, salt, and superfine sugar in a large bowl. Stir in the rhubarb. In a separate bowl mix together the egg, milk, sour cream, and vegetable oil. Add the wet ingredients to the dry ingredients and mix briefly until just combined.

3. Spoon the batter into the prepared muffin cups, then sprinkle with demerara sugar. Bake in the oven for 18–20 minutes, or until well risen and golden. Cool in the pan for 5 minutes, then turn onto a wire rack.

4. While the muffins are baking, finish the Crème Anglaise. Whisk the egg yolks, cornstarch, and sugar together in a bowl until pale and creamy. Remove the vanilla bean from the milk and scrape out the black seeds. Add the seeds to the egg mixture. Reheat the milk to the boiling point, then slowly pour into the egg mixture, whisking all the time. Pour back into the pan.

5. Cook over a very low heat, stirring constantly for 10–15 minutes, or until the mixture thickens enough to coat the back of the spoon; do not allow the mixture to boil. Serve the muffins warm with the Crème Anglaise.

PEANUT BUTTER Muffins

For a pure, unadulterated peanut butter hit, try these mouth-watering muffins accompanied by a glass of cold milk.

MAKES 12

2 cups all-purpose flour
1 1/2 teaspoons baking powder
1/2 teaspoon salt
4 tablespoons finely chopped unsalted, roasted peanuts
1/2 cup light brown sugar
Scant 3/4 cup smooth peanut butter
3/4 cup milk
2 tablespoons vegetable oil
2 eggs, lightly beaten
1 tablespoon demerara sugar

1. Preheat the oven to 375°F. Grease a 12-cup muffin pan or line the cups with paper muffin cups.

2. Mix the flour, baking powder, and salt in a large bowl. Stir in 2 tablespoons of the chopped peanuts and the brown sugar. Add the peanut butter and rub in until the mixture resembles coarse breadcrumbs.

3. In a separate bowl, mix together the milk, vegetable oil, and eggs. Add the wet ingredients all at once to the dry ingredients and mix briefly until just combined.

4. Spoon the batter into the prepared muffin cups, dividing it evenly. Combine the remaining chopped peanuts and demerara sugar, then sprinkle this mixture over the tops of the muffins.

5. Bake in the oven for 16–18 minutes, or until risen and golden. Cool in the pan for 10 minutes, then turn out onto a wire rack. Serve warm or cold.

BUTTER TART Muffins with Raisins & Walnuts

Gooey and buttery, these muffins are reminiscent of Canadian or Scottish butter tarts, which are similar to pecan pie—but without the pecans!

MAKES 12

1¹/₃ cups raisins
³/₄ cup sugar
¹/₂ cup butter
¹/₂ cup milk
1 teaspoon vanilla or rum extract
2 eggs, lightly beaten
2 cups all-purpose flour
2 teaspoons baking powder
1 teaspoon baking soda
Pinch of salt
¹/₂ cup walnuts, chopped
3–4 tablespoons light corn syrup

MUFFIN TIP
*Try using golden raisins
or chopped dried apricots
instead of raisins, and
pecans or pine nuts instead
of walnuts.*

1. Preheat the oven to 375°F. Grease a 12-cup muffin pan or line the cups with paper muffin cups.

2. Combine the raisins, sugar, butter, milk, and vanilla or rum extract in a saucepan. Cook over a medium heat, stirring almost constantly, until the mixture is hot and the sugar has melted. Bring just to a simmer, then remove the pan from the heat. Allow the mixture to cool for 10 minutes, then whisk in the eggs. Set aside to cool until just warm.

3. Mix the flour, baking powder, baking soda, and salt in a large bowl. Make a well in the center and pour in the raisin mixture, stirring briefly until just combined. Gently fold in the walnuts, then spoon the batter into the prepared muffin cups, dividing it evenly. Bake in the oven for 15–17 minutes, or until risen and golden.

4. Remove from the oven and immediately drizzle about 1 teaspoon of corn syrup over the top of each muffin. Cool in the pan for 10 minutes, then turn out onto a wire rack. Serve warm or cold.

STICKY GINGERBREAD Muffins

These tasty muffins make a delicious dessert if served warm with creamy custard sauce. Alternatively, eat them when cold, split and spread with a little butter.

MAKES 10

1³/₄ cups self-rising flour
¹/₂ teaspoon baking soda
¹/₂ teaspoon salt
2 teaspoons ground ginger
1 teaspoon ground cinnamon
Pinch of freshly grated nutmeg
³/₄ cup light brown sugar
2 tablespoons light corn syrup
1 tablespoon molasses
7 tablespoons butter, cut into small
  pieces
³/₄ cup milk
1 egg, lightly beaten

1. Preheat the oven to 375°F. Grease 10 cups of a 12-cup muffin pan or line 10 cups with paper muffin cups.

2. Mix the flour, baking soda, salt, ginger, cinnamon, nutmeg, and sugar in a large bowl.

3. Put the corn syrup, molasses, butter, and about one-third of the milk in a small saucepan. Heat gently until the butter has melted. Stir with a fork until the syrup and molasses are blended, then stir in the rest of the milk, followed by the egg. Add the wet ingredients all at once to the dry ingredients and mix briefly until just combined.

4. Spoon the batter into the prepared muffin cups, dividing it evenly. Bake in the oven for about 20 minutes, or until well risen and firm to the touch. Cool in the pan for 10 minutes, then turn out onto a wire rack. Serve warm or cold.

MUFFIN TIP
To make measuring the syrup and molasses easier, coat your measuring spoon with a little oil. Alternatively, stand the jars in hot water for a few minutes to make the contents thinner and runnier.

CINNAMON & PECAN Muffins

If you can't find buttermilk, simply mix 1 teaspoon of white vinegar into ¾ cup milk and leave at room temperature for 1 hour until slightly curdled.

MAKES 12

2 cups all-purpose flour
1 teaspoon baking powder
1 teaspoon baking soda
Pinch of salt
½ cup butter, softened
Generous ¾ cup superfine sugar
2 eggs, lightly beaten
1 teaspoon vanilla extract
¾ cup buttermilk
6 tablespoons light brown sugar
1 teaspoon ground cinnamon
½ cup pecans, coarsely chopped

1. Preheat the oven to 375°F. Grease a 12-cup muffin pan or line the cups with paper muffin cups.

2. Mix the flour, baking powder, baking soda, and salt in a large bowl. In a separate bowl, cream the butter and superfine sugar together until light and fluffy. Gradually beat in the eggs and vanilla extract. Stir in the buttermilk.

3. Add the wet ingredients all at once to the dry ingredients and mix briefly until just combined. In a small bowl, mix together the brown sugar, cinnamon, and pecans.

4. Spoon half of the batter into the prepared muffin cups, then sprinkle with half of the pecan and cinnamon mixture. Repeat with the remaining batter and pecan mixture, dividing it evenly and gently pressing the pecan mixture into the batter using the back of a spoon.

5. Bake in the oven for 20–25 minutes, or until well risen and firm to the touch. Cool in the pan for 10 minutes, then turn out onto a wire rack. Serve warm or cold.

SUGAR & SPICE
Muffins

Sometimes the simplest muffins are the best. These buttery spiced muffins fill the kitchen with a wonderful aroma as they bake.

MAKES **10**

1³/₄ cups self-rising flour
1 teaspoon baking powder
1 teaspoon ground ginger
1 teaspoon ground cinnamon
¹/₄ teaspoon freshly grated nutmeg
Pinch of ground cloves (optional)
Pinch of salt
²/₃ cup superfine sugar
1 egg, lightly beaten
²/₃ cup milk
6 tablespoons butter, melted

FOR THE TOPPING
2 tablespoons light brown sugar
1 teaspoon ground cinnamon

1. Preheat the oven to 375°F. Grease 10 cups of a 12-cup muffin pan or line 10 cups with paper muffin cups.

2. For the muffins, mix the flour, baking powder, ginger, cinnamon, nutmeg, cloves, salt, and sugar in a large bowl. In a separate bowl, mix together the egg, milk, and melted butter. Add the wet ingredients all at once to the dry ingredients and mix briefly until just combined.

3. Spoon the batter into the prepared muffin cups, dividing it evenly. Mix together the topping ingredients, then sprinkle this mixture over the tops of the muffins. Bake in the oven for 18–20 minutes, or until well risen and golden. Cool in the pan for 5 minutes, then turn out onto a wire rack. Serve warm or cold.

MUFFIN TIP
Pumpkin pie spice, may be used instead of the combination of spices given, if you prefer.

BUTTERED BRAZIL NUT Muffins

Lightly toasting the Brazil nuts in a little butter brings out their unique flavor, making them ideal for these tasty muffins.

MAKES 12

1 cup Brazil nuts, roughly chopped
6 tablespoons butter
Pinch of freshly grated nutmeg
2 cups self-rising flour
1 teaspoon baking powder
1/2 teaspoon baking soda
1/4 teaspoon salt
1/2 cup superfine sugar
1 egg, lightly beaten
1 cup milk
Few drops of almond extract

MUFFIN TIP
Check the muffins after 15 minutes baking time to make sure that the nuts aren't over-browning. If they are sufficiently colored, cover the muffins with a piece of foil for the remaining cooking time.

1. Preheat the oven to 375°F. Grease a 12-cup muffin pan or line the cups with paper muffin cups.

2. Set aside 1/3 cup of the Brazil nuts. Melt 2 tablespoons of the butter in a small non-stick frying pan. Add the remaining chopped Brazil nuts and cook over a low heat for a few minutes until just beginning to turn golden. Remove the pan from the heat, cool for 1 minute, then add the remaining butter and the nutmeg to the pan. Stir until melted, then set aside.

3. Mix the flour, baking powder, baking soda, salt, and sugar in a large bowl. In a separate bowl, mix together the egg, milk, and almond extract. Stir in the toasted Brazil nuts and melted butter mixture. Add the wet ingredients all at once to the dry ingredients and mix briefly until just combined.

4. Spoon the batter into the prepared muffin cups, dividing it evenly, then sprinkle the tops with the reserved Brazil nuts. Bake in the oven for about 20 minutes, or until well risen and firm to the touch. Cool in the pan for 5 minutes, then turn out onto a wire rack. Serve warm or cold.

COCONUT CRUMBLE & RASPBERRY Muffins

A crunchy coconut topping and smooth, tangy raspberry center makes a tasty contrast in these tempting muffins.

MAKES 12

2½ cups all-purpose flour
1 tablespoon baking powder
1 cup dried coconut
1 cup superfine sugar
2 teaspoons finely grated lime zest
2 eggs, lightly beaten
¾ cup milk
¼ cup coconut milk
7 tablespoons butter, melted
4 tablespoons seedless raspberry jelly

FOR THE COCONUT CRUMBLE TOPPING

¼ cup all-purpose flour
½ cup flaked coconut
1 tablespoon superfine sugar
2 tablespoons butter, cut into small
   pieces

1. Preheat the oven to 375°F. Grease a 12-cup non-stick muffin pan.

2. For the coconut crumble topping, place all the ingredients in a small bowl and rub in the butter until the mixture resembles coarse breadcrumbs. Set aside.

3. For the muffins, mix the flour, baking powder, dried coconut, sugar, and lime zest in a large bowl. In a separate bowl, mix together the eggs, milk, coconut milk, and melted butter. Add the wet ingredients all at once to the dry ingredients and mix briefly until just combined.

4. Spoon about half of the batter into the prepared muffin cups. Make a small hollow in each and fill with 1 teaspoon of jelly. Top with the remaining batter, dividing it evenly. Sprinkle the tops with the coconut crumble topping.

5. Bake in the oven for 20 minutes, or until well risen and golden. Cool in the pan for 10 minutes, then turn out onto a wire rack. Serve warm or cold.

MAPLE PECAN Muffins

These are made by first creaming the butter and sugar together, which gives the muffins a lighter and spongier texture.

MAKES 12

1/2 cup butter, softened
2/3 cup superfine sugar
2 tablespoons ground almonds
2 eggs, lightly beaten
1/2 cup pecans, coarsely chopped
2 cups all-purpose flour
1 1/2 teaspoons baking powder
2 teaspoons baking soda
Pinch of salt
3/4 cup buttermilk
7 tablespoons maple syrup
6–12 pecan halves, to decorate

1. Preheat the oven to 375°F. Grease a 12-cup muffin pan or line the cups with paper muffin cups.

2. Cream the butter and sugar together in a bowl until light and fluffy. Stir in the ground almonds, then gradually beat in the eggs. Stir in the chopped pecans.

3. Sift the flour, baking powder, baking soda, and salt into the creamed mixture. In a small bowl, blend the buttermilk with 4 tablespoons of the maple syrup. Pour the buttermilk mixture all at once into the flour and creamed mixture, and mix briefly until just combined.

4. Spoon the batter into the prepared muffin cups, dividing it evenly, then top each muffin with a pecan half. Bake in the oven for about 20 minutes, or until well risen and firm to the touch.

5. Cool in the pan for 5 minutes, then turn out onto a wire rack. Brush or drizzle the remaining 3 tablespoons of maple syrup over the hot baked muffins and serve warm or cold.

MUFFIN TIP
Use real maple syrup for these muffins rather than artificial maple-flavored syrup.

PEAR & GINGER Muffins

If you prefer classic gingerbread muffins, leave the pears and pecans
out of the muffin batter mixture.

MAKES 12

Generous 1 cup margarine, softened
Generous 1/2 cup superfine sugar
Scant 1/4 cup molasses
2 eggs, lightly beaten
1 teaspoon baking soda
3/4 cup buttermilk
2 cups all-purpose flour
2 teaspoons ground ginger
1/2 teaspoon ground cinnamon
1/2 teaspoon ground cloves
1/2 cup pecans, chopped
2 ripe pears, peeled, cored, and finely
   chopped

MUFFIN TIP
*Use 2 apples
instead of the pears if
you would like to
modify this recipe.*

1. Preheat the oven to 350°F. Grease a 12-cup muffin pan or line the
cups with paper muffin cups.

2. Cream the margarine and sugar together in a bowl until light and
fluffy. Stir in the molasses. Beat in the eggs one at a time, beating well
after each addition.

3. In a separate small bowl, gently stir the baking soda into the
buttermilk until it has dissolved.

4. In a separate medium bowl, mix the flour with the ginger, cinnamon,
and cloves, then add the flour mixture to the creamed mixture alternately
with the buttermilk. Fold in the pecans and pears.

5. Spoon the batter into the prepared muffin cups, dividing it evenly.
Bake in the oven for about 20 minutes, or until risen and firm to the
touch. Cool in the pan for 10 minutes, then turn out onto a wire rack.
Serve warm or cold.

PUMPKIN, MAPLE SYRUP & WALNUT Muffins

Pumpkin purée, maple syrup, and walnuts combine well to create these delicious moist muffins, ideal for Halloween.

MAKES 12

2 cups all-purpose flour

2 teaspoons baking powder

1/2 teaspoon baking soda

1 teaspoon ground cinnamon

1/2 teaspoon freshly grated nutmeg

1/4 teaspoon salt

3/4 cup light brown sugar

1/2 cup walnuts, chopped

2 eggs, lightly beaten

Generous 1 cup pumpkin purée (fresh or canned)

3/4 cup evaporated milk

3 tablespoons vegetable oil

1 tablespoon maple syrup

FOR THE TOPPING

1 tablespoon light brown sugar

1/4 cup walnuts, chopped

FOR THE FILLING

1/3 cup cream cheese, softened

2 tablespoons light brown sugar

2 tablespoons maple syrup

1. Preheat the oven to 400°F. Grease a 12-cup muffin pan or line the cups with paper muffin cups.

2. For the filling, mix together the cream cheese, sugar, and maple syrup in a bowl until smooth. Set aside.

3. For the muffins, mix the flour, baking powder, baking soda, cinnamon, nutmeg, and salt in a large bowl. Stir in the sugar and walnuts. In a separate bowl, mix together the eggs, pumpkin purée, evaporated milk, vegetable oil, and maple syrup.

4. Add the wet ingredients all at once to the dry ingredients and mix briefly until just combined. Add the cheese filling to the batter and swirl through the mixture with a knife until the batter looks marbled. For the topping, mix together the sugar and walnuts in a small bowl.

5. Spoon the batter into the prepared muffin cups, dividing it evenly, then sprinkle the tops with the topping mixture. Bake in the oven for about 20 minutes, or until risen and golden. Cool in the pan for 10 minutes, then turn out onto a wire rack. Serve warm or cold.

ROSEMARY & BAY-SCENTED Muffins

Here, the subtle fragrance of rosemary and bay leaves is complemented by a sweet orange glaze to create these delicious muffins.

MAKES 10

1 tender fresh rosemary sprig, about 4 inches long
2 dried bay leaves
Small strip of pared orange rind
²/₃ cup milk
1 tablespoon cold water
1³/₄ cup self-rising flour
1 teaspoon baking powder
Pinch of salt
²/₃ cup superfine sugar
1 egg, lightly beaten
7 tablespoons butter, melted

FOR THE ORANGE GLAZE & DECORATION

1¹/₂ cups powdered sugar
Finely grated zest of ¹/₂ orange
About 1¹/₂–2 tablespoons unsweetened orange juice
Tiny fresh rosemary sprigs, to decorate (optional)

1. For the muffins, rinse the rosemary and bay leaves in cold water, then put them in a small saucepan with the pared orange rind, milk, and water. Slowly bring the mixture to the boil, then remove the pan from the heat, cover with a lid, and leave to infuse and cool for 20 minutes. Discard the herbs and orange rind.

2. Preheat the oven to 375°F. Grease 10 cups of a 12-cup muffin pan or line 10 cups with paper muffin cups.

3. Mix the flour, baking powder, salt, and sugar in a large bowl. Stir the egg and melted butter into the herb-infused milk. Add the milk mixture all at once to the dry ingredients and mix briefly until just combined.

4. Spoon the batter into the prepared muffin cups, dividing evenly. Bake in the oven for 18–20 minutes, or until well risen and golden. Cool in the pan for 5 minutes, then turn onto a wire rack to cool completely.

5. For the orange glaze, sift the powdered sugar into a bowl. Add the orange zest, then stir in 1¹/₂ tablespoons of orange juice, adding a little more if necessary to make a smooth, fairly thin icing or glaze. Spoon the glaze over the tops of the muffins and decorate with tiny rosemary sprig, if you like, before serving.

SAVORY MUFFINS

BACON & CREAMY CORN Muffins

These are a variation on the popular corn muffin. They're great for breakfast or for a light lunch, served with a little green salad on the side.

MAKES 12

8 ounces sliced bacon rashers
1 small onion, finely chopped
1 cup all-purpose flour
1¼ cups cornmeal or instant polenta
2 tablespoons superfine sugar
4 teaspoons baking powder
½ teaspoon salt
Scant 1 cup canned cream-style corn
½ cup milk
1 egg, lightly beaten

1. Preheat the oven to 400°F. Grease a 12-cup muffin pan or line the cups with paper muffin cups.

2. Cook the bacon in a large frying pan (or under a preheated broiler) until crisp. Remove the bacon from the pan and drain well on paper towels. Add the onion to the same pan and sauté for about 5–7 minutes, or until soft and lightly golden. Remove the onion from the pan. Break or chop the bacon into small pieces and set aside with the onion. Reserve about 3 tablespoons of the bacon fat (or substitute vegetable oil).

3. Mix the flour, cornmeal or polenta, sugar, baking powder, and salt in a bowl. In a separate bowl, beat together the corn, milk, egg, and reserved bacon fat (or vegetable oil). Add the corn mixture to the flour mixture and mix briefly until just combined. Fold in the reserved bacon and onion.

4. Spoon the batter into the prepared muffin cups, dividing it evenly. Bake in the oven for about 20 minutes, or until golden. Cool in the pan for 5 minutes, then carefully turn out onto a wire rack. These muffins are best served warm from the oven.

CAJUN-SPICED CORN Muffins

These muffins smell wonderful as they are baking and are a great accompaniment to any Cajun-style stew or fish dish.

MAKES 12

1¼ cups cornmeal or instant polenta
1 cup all-purpose flour
1 tablespoon superfine sugar
1 tablespoon baking powder
1 teaspoon salt
½ teaspoon baking soda
½ teaspoon Cajun spice mix
¾ cup buttermilk
2 eggs, lightly beaten
½ cup frozen corn kernels
2 scallions, finely chopped
2 tablespoons vegetable oil
¼ teaspoon Tabasco sauce
   (or to taste)

1. Preheat the oven to 400°F. Grease a 12-cup muffin pan or line the cups with paper muffin cups.

2. Mix the cornmeal or polenta, flour, sugar, baking powder, salt, baking soda, and Cajun spice mix in a large bowl.

3. In a separate bowl, mix together the buttermilk, eggs, corn, scallions, vegetable oil, and Tabasco sauce. Add the wet ingredients all at once to the dry ingredients and mix briefly until just combined.

4. Spoon the batter into the prepared muffin cups, dividing it evenly. Bake in the oven for 18–20 minutes, or until well risen and golden. Cool in the pan for 5 minutes, then turn out onto a wire rack. Serve warm.

FRESH TOMATO & MIXED OLIVE Muffins

A crunchy crumb, Parmesan, and poppy seed topping adds the final touch to these delicious savory muffins.

MAKES 12

2 cups all-purpose flour
1 tablespoon baking powder
1 tablespoon superfine sugar
1/4 cup fresh Parmesan cheese, finely grated
3 tablespoons chopped fresh basil
1 egg, lightly beaten
3/4 cup milk
Scant 1/2 cup butter, melted
1 tablespoon olive oil
4 medium ripe tomatoes, skinned, seeded and chopped
1/3 cup pitted mixed black and green olives, roughly chopped
1 clove garlic, crushed
Salt and freshly ground black pepper, to taste

FOR THE TOPPING
3/4 cup breadcrumbs
1/4 cup fresh Parmesan cheese, finely grated
2 teaspoons poppy seeds

1. Preheat the oven to 400°F. Grease a 12-cup muffin pan or line the cups with paper muffin cups.

2. For the muffins, mix the flour, baking powder, sugar, Parmesan cheese, and basil in a large bowl. In a separate bowl, mix together the egg, milk, melted butter, olive oil, tomatoes, olives, garlic, salt, and pepper. Pour the tomato mixture into the dry ingredients and mix until just combined.

3. Spoon the batter into the prepared muffin cups, dividing it evenly. For the topping, stir together the breadcrumbs, Parmesan cheese, and poppy seeds. Sprinkle this mixture over the tops of the muffins.

4. Bake in the oven for about 20 minutes, or until well risen and lightly browned. Cool in the pan for 5 minutes, then turn out onto a wire rack. Serve warm or cold.

MEDITERRANEAN Muffins

These savory muffins would make a delicious light lunch served
with a simple green salad.

MAKES 12

Scant 1³/₄ cups self-rising flour

³/₄ cup cornmeal or instant polenta,
  plus extra for sprinkling

1 teaspoon baking powder

2 teaspoons superfine sugar

¹/₄ teaspoon salt

¹/₃ cup fresh Parmesan cheese,
  finely grated

1 tablespoon chopped fresh herbs
  such as thyme, oregano, or
  rosemary

2 tablespoons fresh basil leaves, torn
  into small pieces

4 scallions, thinly sliced

¹/₄ cup toasted pine nuts

2 eggs, lightly beaten

5 tablespoons olive oil

²/₃ cup milk

²/₃ cup plain yogurt

1. Preheat the oven to 375°F. Grease a 12-cup muffin pan or line the
cups with paper muffin cups.

2. Mix the flour, cornmeal or polenta, baking powder, sugar, salt,
Parmesan cheese, herbs, scallions, and pine nuts in a large bowl. In a
separate bowl, mix together the eggs, olive oil, milk, and yogurt. Add the
wet ingredients to the dry ingredients and mix until just combined.

3. Spoon the batter into the prepared muffin cups, dividing it evenly, then
sprinkle the tops with a little cornmeal or polenta. Bake in the oven for
about 20 minutes, or until well risen and firm to the touch. Cool in the
pan for 5 minutes, then turn out onto a wire rack. Serve warm or cold.

MUFFIN TIP
*If using fresh rosemary,
choose young tender
sprigs and use only the
leaves stripped off the
woody stem.*

CHEESE & SUN-DRIED TOMATO Muffins

Sun-dried tomatoes have a wonderfully concentrated flavor and have a natural affinity with salty olives, pungent garlic, and oregano.

MAKES 10

2 cups all-purpose flour

1 tablespoon baking powder

1 tablespoon superfine sugar

1⅓ cups grated mozzarella or cheddar cheese

5 tablespoons olive oil

2 eggs, lightly beaten

½ cup milk

2 cloves garlic, crushed

⅓ cup sun-dried tomatoes (drained if in oil), chopped

⅓ cup pitted black olives, roughly chopped

2 teaspoons chopped fresh or 1 teaspoon dried oregano

Salt and freshly ground black pepper, to taste

1. Preheat the oven to 375°F. Grease 10 cups of a 12-cup muffin pan or line 10 cups with paper muffin cups.

2. Mix the flour, baking powder, sugar, and mozzarella or cheddar cheese in a large bowl. In a separate bowl, mix together the olive oil, eggs, and milk. Stir in the garlic, sun-dried tomatoes, olives, oregano, a little salt, and some black pepper to taste. Add the wet ingredients to the dry ingredients and mix briefly until just combined.

3. Spoon the batter into the prepared muffin cups, dividing it evenly. Bake in the oven for about 20 minutes, or until well risen and firm to the touch. Cool in the pan for 5 minutes, then turn out onto a wire rack. Serve warm or cold.

MUFFIN TIP

If the sun-dried tomatoes aren't moist, soak them for about 10 minutes in the milk and oil mixture before adding to the dry ingredients.

CHEESY DOUBLE CORN Muffins

These tasty muffins are fabulous served with a hot bowl of spicy chili con carne or fresh tomato soup.

MAKES 12

³/₄ cup all-purpose flour
1¹/₄ cups cornmeal or instant polenta
1 teaspoon baking soda
1 teaspoon baking powder
2 teaspoons salt
¹/₄ cup margarine
³/₄ cup cheddar cheese, grated
2 eggs, lightly beaten
1 cup milk
Scant 1 cup canned cream-style corn

1. Preheat the oven to 400°F. Grease a 12-cup muffin pan or line the cups with paper muffin cups.

2. Mix the flour, cornmeal or polenta, baking soda, baking powder, and salt in a large bowl. Rub in the margarine until the mixture resembles coarse breadcrumbs. Stir in the cheddar cheese.

3. In a separate bowl, mix together the eggs and milk. Add the egg mixture to the dry ingredients, together with the corn and mix briefly until just combined.

4. Spoon the batter into the prepared muffin cups, dividing it evenly. Bake in the oven for 20–25 minutes, or until risen and golden. Cool in the pan for 10 minutes, then turn out onto a wire rack. These muffins are best served on the day they are baked, warm from the oven if possible.

MUFFIN TIP
Most muffins can be frozen for up to 3 months and will take about 30 minutes to thaw at room temperature or just a few seconds in the microwave.

PLANTAIN & HERB Muffins

Plantains can be eaten at every stage of ripeness but must be cooked. When green, their flavor and texture is akin to potato; when ripe (and black), they are more similar to the bananas they resemble, becoming sweet and soft.

MAKES 12

2 cups all-purpose flour
1 tablespoon baking powder
1 teaspoon baking soda
1 teaspoon salt
1 tablespoon chopped fresh thyme leaves
1 tablespoon chopped fresh chives
1 tablespoon chopped fresh parsley
1 clove garlic, crushed
³/₄ cup plain yogurt
²/₃ cup milk
2 eggs, lightly beaten
2 tablespoons vegetable oil
1 tablespoon horseradish sauce
1 large green plantain, peeled and grated

1. Preheat the oven to 400°F. Grease a 12-cup muffin pan or line the cups with paper muffin cups.

2. Mix the flour, baking powder, baking soda, and salt in a large bowl. Add the thyme, chives, parsley, and garlic and mix well.

3. In a separate bowl, mix together the yogurt, milk, eggs, and vegetable oil. Add the wet ingredients all at once to the dry ingredients, together with the horseradish sauce and grated plantain, and mix briefly until just combined.

4. Spoon the batter into the prepared muffin cups, dividing it evenly. Bake in the oven for 20–25 minutes, or until risen and golden. Cool in the pan for 10 minutes, then turn out onto a wire rack. Serve warm or cold.

HOT CHILI & CORN
Muffins

These colorful spicy muffins would be excellent served with a Mexican-style soup.

MAKES 12

1 cup all-purpose flour
1¹/₂ cups cornmeal or instant polenta
Scant ¹/₂ cup superfine sugar
1 tablespoon baking powder
¹/₂ teaspoon salt
1 egg, lightly beaten
2 tablespoons butter, melted
2 tablespoons olive oil
³/₄ cup milk
1 small red pepper, seeded and
    chopped
1 fresh green chili, seeded and finely
    chopped
8-ounce can corn kernels, drained
¹/₂ teaspoon ground paprika

1. Preheat the oven to 400°F. Grease a 12-cup muffin pan or line the cups with paper muffin cups.

2. Mix the flour, cornmeal or polenta, sugar, baking powder, and salt in a large bowl. In a separate bowl, mix together the egg, melted butter, olive oil, milk, red pepper, chili, and corn. Pour the corn mixture into the dry ingredients and mix briefly until just combined.

3. Spoon the batter into the prepared muffin cups, dividing it evenly, then lightly dust the tops with paprika. Bake in the oven for about 20 minutes, or until well risen and lightly browned. Cool in the pan for 5 minutes, then turn out onto a wire rack. Serve warm or cold.

MUFFIN TIP
For even spicier muffins, add ¹/₂ teaspoon hot chilli powder to the dry ingredients.

COTTAGE CHEESE & CHIVE Muffins

These savory muffins would make a very nice light lunch, served with some soup and perhaps a side salad.

MAKES 12

2 cups self-rising flour
$^1/_2$ teaspoon baking powder
$^1/_2$ teaspoon baking soda
$^1/_2$ teaspoon salt
$^1/_4$ cup butter, softened
$^1/_4$ cup light brown sugar
1 egg, lightly beaten
Generous 1 cup cottage cheese
$^1/_4$ cup skim milk
3 tablespoons chopped fresh chives

1. Preheat the oven to 375°F. Grease a 12-cup muffin pan or line the cups with paper muffin cups.

2. Mix the flour, baking powder, baking soda, and salt in a large bowl. In a separate bowl, cream the butter and sugar together until light and fluffy. Beat in the egg. Add the cottage cheese and milk and stir until well mixed. Add the cottage cheese mixture to the dry ingredients, together with the chives and mix briefly until just combined.

3. Spoon the batter into the prepared muffin cups, dividing it evenly. Bake in the oven for about 20 minutes, or until risen and golden. Cool in the pan for 10 minutes, then turn out onto a wire rack. Serve warm or cold.

MUFFIN TIP
You could try using flavored cottage cheese for this recipe if you like, but make sure that the added ingredients do not change the consistency.

SAUSAGE & CHEESE Muffins

Use the best quality sausages you can afford, as they are the predominant flavor in these tasty muffins.

MAKES 12

8 ounces good-quality ground pork sausage
1 small onion, grated
2 cups all-purpose flour
2 tablespoons superfine sugar
1 tablespoon baking powder
1/4 teaspoon salt
3/4 cup milk
1 large egg, lightly beaten
1/4 cup butter, melted
1/2 cup cheddar cheese, grated

1. Preheat the oven to 375°F. Grease a 12-cup muffin pan or line the cups with paper muffin cups.

2. Cook the sausage in a large skillet over a high heat for 8–10 minutes, or until cooked through and golden, breaking up the sausage with a wooden spoon as it cooks. Remove the sausage from the pan and drain on paper towels, then set aside. Add the onion to the pan and sauté for 3–4 minutes, or until softened. Remove the onion to a plate and set aside.

3. Mix the flour, sugar, baking powder, and salt in a large bowl. In a separate bowl, mix together the milk, egg, and melted butter. Add the egg mixture all at once to the dry ingredients, together with the cheddar cheese, sausage, and onion. Mix briefly until just combined.

4. Spoon the batter into the prepared muffin cups, dividing it evenly. Bake in the oven for about 20 minutes, or until well risen and golden. Cool in the pan for 10 minutes, then turn out onto a wire rack. These muffins are best served warm.

BEER & ONION
Muffins

This unlikely combination works really well in these muffins
—creating the perfect partner to an afternoon watching
football or your favorite film.

MAKES 12

2 cups all-purpose flour
2 tablespoons superfine sugar
1 tablespoon baking powder
1 teaspoon salt
$\frac{1}{2}$ teaspoon freshly ground black
   pepper
$\frac{1}{2}$ teaspoon garlic powder
1 cup beer, allowed to go flat and at
   room temperature
$\frac{1}{2}$ cup vegetable oil
1 egg, lightly beaten
1 small onion, grated
1 tablespoon chopped fresh thyme
   leaves

1. Preheat the oven to 400°F. Grease a 12-cup muffin pan or line the
cups with paper muffin cups.

2. Mix the flour, sugar, baking powder, salt, pepper, and garlic powder in a
large bowl.

3. In a separate bowl, whisk together the beer, vegetable oil, egg, onion,
and thyme. Add the wet ingredients all at once to the dry ingredients and
mix briefly until just combined.

4. Spoon the batter into the prepared muffin cups, dividing it evenly.
Bake in the oven for 20–25 minutes, or until
risen and golden. Cool in the pan for
10 minutes, then turn out onto a
wire rack. Serve warm.

MUFFIN TIP
*Always bake muffins as
soon as you've filled the pans,
on the middle oven shelf or just
a little higher. Close the oven
door as quickly as possible to
prevent heat from
being lost.*

CHEESE & ONION Muffins

These are deeply savory muffins that go really well with soups or stews.

MAKES 12

4 tablespoons vegetable oil
1 large onion, coarsely chopped
2 cups all-purpose flour
$3/4$ cup mature cheddar cheese, grated
1 tablespoon baking powder
1 teaspoon onion salt
1 cup milk
2 large eggs, lightly beaten

1. Preheat the oven to 350°F. Grease a 12-cup muffin pan or line the cups with paper muffin cups.

2. Heat 1 tablespoon of the vegetable oil in a skillet, add the onion, and sauté over a medium heat for 8–10 minutes, or until crisp and golden. Remove the onion from the pan and drain on paper towels, then set aside to cool.

3. Mix the flour, fried onion, cheddar cheese, baking powder, and onion salt in a large bowl. In a separate bowl, mix together the milk, eggs, and the remaining vegetable oil. Add the wet ingredients all at once to the dry ingredients and mix briefly until just combined.

4. Spoon the batter into the prepared muffin cups, dividing it evenly. Bake in the oven for 15–18 minutes, or until risen and golden. Cool in the pan for 10 minutes, then turn out onto a wire rack. Serve warm.

CRUMBLE-TOPPED BACON & CHEDDAR Muffins

These smoky bacon and cheese muffins have a tasty savory crumble topping. They're best eaten while still warm.

MAKES 12

4 ounces sliced smoked bacon
1 cup self-rising flour
1 cup self-rising whole-wheat flour
1 teaspoon superfine sugar
1 teaspoon baking powder
1/2 teaspoon dry English mustard
1 cup cheddar cheese, grated
4 tablespoons chopped fresh parsley
Freshly ground black pepper, to taste
1 egg, lightly beaten
1 1/4 cups milk
6 tablespoons butter, melted

FOR THE CRUMBLE TOPPING

2 tablespoons butter
1/4 cup all-purpose flour
1/4 cup cheddar cheese, finely grated

1. Preheat the oven to 400°F. Grease a 12-cup non-stick muffin pan. For the crumble topping, rub the butter into the flour in a bowl until the mixture resembles fine breadcrumbs. Stir in the cheddar cheese. Set aside.

2. For the muffins, fry the bacon in a non-stick skillet until golden brown and crispy. Remove the bacon from the pan and drain on paper towels. Leave to cool, then break or chop the bacon into small pieces.

3. Mix the flours, sugar, baking powder, and mustard in a large bowl. Stir in the cheddar cheese, parsley, and bacon and season to taste with black pepper. In a separate bowl, mix together the egg, milk, and melted butter. Pour the wet ingredients into the dry ingredients and mix briefly until just combined.

4. Spoon the batter into the prepared muffin cups, dividing it evenly, then sprinkle the tops with the crumble mixture. Bake in the oven for about 20 minutes, or until well risen and lightly browned. Cool in the pan for 5 minutes, then turn out onto a wire rack. Serve warm or cold.

DOUBLE CHEESE & CHIVE Muffins

The mild onion taste of fresh chives enhances the flavor of the cheeses in these savory muffins.

MAKES 12

2 cups all-purpose flour
1 tablespoon baking powder
1 tablespoon superfine sugar
1/4 teaspoon salt
6 tablespoons butter
1/4 cup fresh Parmesan cheese,
   finely grated
Generous 1/4 cup cheddar cheese, cut
   into tiny cubes
2 tablespoons chopped fresh chives
1 egg, lightly beaten
1 cup milk

MUFFIN TIP
*Scatter the cheese
cubes in the middle and
not towards the edges of the
muffins, as they may over-
brown and stick to
the pan.*

1. Preheat the oven to 375°F. Grease a 12-cup non-stick muffin pan.

2. Put the flour, baking powder, sugar, and salt in a large bowl. Cut the butter into small pieces and rub into the flour mixture until the mixture resembles fine breadcrumbs. Reserve 2 tablespoons of the Parmesan cheese and 2 tablespoons of the cheddar cheese. Stir the rest of each type of cheese into the flour mixture, together with the chives.

3. In a separate bowl, mix together the egg and milk. Add the egg mixture all at once to the dry ingredients and mix until just combined.

4. Spoon the batter into the prepared muffin cups, dividing it evenly, then sprinkle the tops with the reserved cheddar cheese cubes. Scatter a little of the remaining Parmesan cheese on top of each muffin. Bake in the oven for 18–20 minutes, or until risen and golden. Cool in the pan for 10 minutes, then turn out onto a wire rack. Serve warm or cold.

PUMPKIN & CHEESE
Muffins

Crunchy and cheesy, these delicious muffins are perfect
for a buffet or light lunch.

MAKES 12

2 cups all-purpose flour
1 tablespoon baking powder
1 teaspoon baking soda
1 teaspoon salt
1 cup firm goat cheese,
   coarsely diced
4 tablespoons toasted pumpkin seeds
Scant 1 cup pumpkin purée (fresh or
   canned)
³/₄ cup plain yogurt
2 eggs, lightly beaten
2 tablespoons vegetable oil

1. Preheat the oven to 400°F. Grease a 12-cup muffin pan or line the
cups with paper muffin cups.

2. Mix the flour, baking powder, baking soda, and salt in a large bowl. Stir
in the goat cheese. Coarsely chop 2 tablespoons of the pumpkin seeds
and set aside the remainder. Stir the chopped pumpkin seeds into the
flour mixture.

3. In a separate bowl, whisk together the pumpkin purée, yogurt, eggs,
and vegetable oil. Add the wet ingredients all at once to the dry
ingredients and mix briefly until just combined.

4. Spoon the batter into the prepared muffin cups, dividing it evenly,
then sprinkle the tops with the remaining pumpkin seeds. Bake in the
oven for 20–25 minutes, or until risen and golden. Cool in the pan for
10 minutes, then turn out onto a wire rack. Serve warm.

SWEET POTATO, ROASTED CHILI & FETA Muffins

MAKES 12

1 medium orange-fleshed sweet
  potato
1 fresh hot red chili
2 cups all-purpose flour
1 tablespoon baking powder
$\frac{1}{2}$ teaspoon salt
1 clove garlic, crushed
1 teaspoon cumin seeds, toasted and
  lightly crushed
1 tablespoon chopped fresh basil
2 eggs, lightly beaten
1 cup milk
3 tablespoons olive oil, plus extra for
  brushing
$\frac{3}{4}$ cup feta cheese, crumbled

1. Preheat the oven to 400°F. Grease a 12-cup muffin pan or line the cups with paper muffin cups.

2. Prick the sweet potato several times with a fork and place it on a small baking sheet or a piece of foil. Bake in the oven for 30–45 minutes, or until tender. Remove from the oven and set aside until cool enough to handle. Once cool, scoop out and mash the flesh. Set aside.

3. Brush the chili with a little olive oil and place under a preheated broiler or over a naked flame, turning frequently, until it is scorched and blackened all over. Put the hot chili into a small paper or plastic food bag and leave until cool enough to handle. Peel the chili, removing all the blackened skin, then slit the chili open lengthways and remove the stem, seeds and membranes. Finely chop the chili flesh. Set aside.

4. Mix the flour, baking powder, and salt in a large bowl. Stir in the garlic, cumin, and basil. In a separate bowl, beat together the eggs, milk, olive oil, and mashed sweet potato. Add the egg mixture all at once to the dry ingredients, together with the chopped chili. Fold in the feta cheese, mixing until just combined.

5. Spoon the batter into the prepared muffin cups, dividing it evenly. Bake in the oven for 20–25 minutes, or until well risen and golden. Cool in the pan for 10 minutes, then turn out onto a wire rack. These muffins are best served warm.

PIZZA Muffins

Combining all the great flavors of a pizza, but more compact,

these pizza muffins make a tasty snack, ideal for lunch or brunch.

MAKES 12

5 tablespoons olive oil

Generous 1 cup mushrooms, sliced

3/4 cup pepperoni, chopped

1/2 cup lean cooked ham, chopped

1 onion, grated

1 1/3 cups grated mozzarella cheese

1/3 cup sun-dried tomatoes (drained if in oil), chopped

1 tablespoon crushed garlic

2 teaspoons chopped fresh or 1 teaspoon dried oregano

1 tablespoon chopped fresh basil

2 eggs, lightly beaten

1/2 cup milk

Salt and freshly ground black pepper, to taste

2 cups all-purpose flour

1 tablespoon baking powder

1. Preheat the oven to 375°F. Grease a 12-cup muffin pan or line the cups with paper muffin cups.

2. Heat 1 1/2 tablespoons of the olive oil in a large skillet. Add the mushrooms and cook over a high heat for about 5 minutes, stirring frequently, until the mushrooms are golden and tender. Remove the pan from the heat and set aside to cool.

3. Mix the pepperoni, ham, onion, mozzarella cheese, sun-dried tomatoes, garlic, oregano, basil, and cooled mushrooms in a bowl.

4. In a separate bowl, mix together the eggs, milk, and remaining olive oil, then add this to the pepperoni mixture. Season to taste with salt and pepper.

5. Mix the flour and baking powder in a separate large bowl. Add the pepperoni mixture and mix briefly until just combined.

6. Spoon the batter into the prepared muffin cups, dividing it evenly. Bake in the oven for 20–25 minutes, or until risen and golden. Cool in the pan for 10 minutes, then turn out onto a wire rack. These muffins are best served warm.

SMOKED BACON & BLUE CHEESE *Muffins*

It's very important to drain the bacon well after frying so that it remains crisp and tasty for these choice muffins.

MAKES 12

8 ounces sliced smoked bacon
2 cups all-purpose flour
1 tablespoon baking powder
$1/2$ teaspoon salt
Generous $1/3$ cup superfine sugar
1 egg, lightly beaten
5 tablespoons water
$3/4$ cup milk
About 10 fresh basil leaves, finely
   chopped
$3/4$ cup blue cheese, crumbled
$1/2$ cup walnuts, chopped

1. Preheat the oven to 350°F. Grease a 12-cup muffin pan or line the cups with paper muffin cups.

2. Fry the bacon in a large skillet until crisp. Remove the bacon from the pan and drain on paper towels. Set aside to cool. Reserve about 5 tablespoons of the bacon fat (or substitute vegetable oil). Break or chop the bacon into small pieces and set aside.

3. Mix the flour, baking powder, salt, and sugar in a large bowl. In a separate bowl, mix together the reserved bacon fat (or vegetable oil), egg, water, and milk. Add the wet ingredients all at once to the dry ingredients, together with the bacon, basil, blue cheese, and walnuts, and mix briefly until just combined.

4. Spoon the batter into the prepared muffin cups, dividing it evenly. Bake in the oven for 20–25 minutes, or until risen and golden. Cool in the pan for 10 minutes, then turn out onto a wire rack. Serve warm.

MINI SEEDED Muffins

These little savory muffins are packed with crunchy seeds. If you like, toast the seeds for a few minutes in a non-stick skillet before using, to bring out their nutty flavor.

MAKES 18

1 1/2 cups self-rising flour
1/4 cup cornmeal or instant polenta
1/2 teaspoon baking powder
1/2 teaspoon dried mixed herbs
1/4 cup sunflower seeds
2 tablespoons pumpkin seeds
1 tablespoon sesame seeds, plus
   2 teaspoons
Salt and freshly ground black pepper,
   to taste
1 egg, lightly beaten
2 1/2 tablespoons olive oil
2/3 cup milk

1. Preheat the oven to 375°F. Grease one 12-cup non-stick mini muffin pan and one 6-cup non-stick mini muffin pan, or grease 18 cups of a 24-cup non-stick mini muffin pan. Alternatively, line the cups with paper muffin cups.

2. Mix the flour, cornmeal or polenta, baking powder, dried herbs, sunflower seeds, pumpkin seeds, and 1 tablespoon of sesame seeds in a large bowl. Season generously with salt and pepper. In a separate bowl, mix together the egg, olive oil, and milk. Add the wet ingredients to the dry ingredients and mix briefly until just combined.

3. Spoon the batter into the prepared muffin cups, dividing it evenly, then sprinkle the tops with the remaining 2 teaspoons of sesame seeds. Bake in the oven for about 10 minutes, or until well risen and golden brown. Cool in the pan for 5 minutes, then turn out onto a wire rack.

Serve warm or cold.

MUFFIN TIP
These mini muffins are delicious with added cheese. Stir 1/2 cup finely grated mature cheddar cheese or 1/4 cup finely grated fresh Parmesan cheese into the dry ingredients.

HEALTHY & SPECIAL DIET
MUFFINS

CINNAMON-SPICED ZUCCHINI Muffins

Choose smaller, firm zucchini rather than larger specimens for these muffins, as they will be less watery and will give a better end result.

MAKES 12

2 cups whole-wheat flour
1/2 cup light brown sugar
1 1/2 tablespoons baking powder
1/2 teaspoon salt
1 teaspoon ground cinnamon
3/4 cup milk
2 eggs, lightly beaten
3 tablespoons sunflower oil
3 tablespoons clear honey
Generous 1/2 cup zucchini, grated

1. Preheat the oven to 375°F. Grease a 12-cup muffin pan or line the cups with paper muffin cups.

2. Mix the flour, sugar, baking powder, salt, and cinnamon in a large bowl.

3. In a separate bowl, mix together the milk, eggs, sunflower oil, honey, and zucchini. Add the wet ingredients all at once to the dry ingredients and mix briefly until just combined.

4. Spoon the batter into the prepared muffin cups, dividing it evenly. Bake in the oven for about 20 minutes, or until risen and lightly browned. Cool in the pan for 10 minutes, then turn out onto a wire rack. Serve warm.

MUFFIN TIP
If grated zucchini seems very watery, drain it on paper towels before adding it to the muffin mix.

SOUR CREAM & RAISIN Muffins

The batter for this classic muffin can be prepared ahead of time and kept in the refrigerator for up to one weeks, if you like. The recipe is also easily halved.

MAKES 36

1 cup boiling water
5 teaspoons baking soda
1 cup margarine
2 cups superfine sugar
2 eggs, lightly beaten
2 tablespoons molasses
5 cups all-purpose flour
4$\frac{1}{2}$ cups toasted bran sticks, such as
   All-Bran cereal
2 cups bran flakes
2 cups raisins
1 tablespoon salt
4 cups buttermilk

1. Preheat the oven to 400°F. Grease three 12-cup muffin pans (or however many muffin cups you wish to use, see recipe introduction) or line the cups with paper muffin cups.

2. Pour the boiling water over the baking soda in a very large bowl. Stir until dissolved, then set aside to cool. In a separate bowl, cream the margarine and sugar together until light and fluffy, then gradually beat in the eggs. Stir in the molasses. In another bowl, mix together the flour, bran cereal, bran flakes, raisins, and salt.

3. Add the buttermilk to the baking soda mixture. Add about half of the wet and dry ingredients alternately to the creamed mixture, stirring briefly to mix. Add the remaining wet and dry ingredients, mixing briefly until just combined.

4. Spoon the batter into the prepared muffin cups, dividing it evenly. Bake in the oven for about 20 minutes, or until risen and firm to the touch. Cool in the pan for 10 minutes, then turn out onto a wire rack. Serve warm or cold, split, and spread with a little sunflower margarine.

BUTTERMILK BRAN Muffins

Contrary to its name, buttermilk is a low-fat product, which adds a unique flavor and lightness to muffins. Use your favorite dried fruit in these; golden raisins, cranberries, blueberries, chopped dates, or apricots all work well.

MUFFIN TIP
The muffin batter will be fairly wet when spooned into the muffin cups, but the oat bran and dried fruit will soak up a lot of moisture as the muffins bake.

MAKES 12

1³/₄ cups all-purpose flour

Scant 1 cup oat bran, or a mixture of oat bran and oat germ

1 tablespoon baking powder

¹/₂ teaspoon salt

³/₄ cup light brown sugar

¹/₂ cup dried fruit, such as golden raisins, cranberries or chopped (pitted) dates

1 egg, lightly beaten

1 cup buttermilk

4 tablespoons milk or unsweetened orange, apple, or other fruit juice

1 tablespoon clear honey or molasses

6 tablespoons sunflower oil

1. Preheat the oven to 375°F. Grease a 12-cup muffin pan or line the cups with paper muffin cups.

2. Mix the flour, oat bran, baking powder, salt, sugar, and dried fruit in a large bowl. In a separate bowl, mix together the egg, buttermilk, milk or fruit juice, honey or molasses, and sunflower oil. Add the buttermilk mixture all at once to the dry ingredients and mix briefly until just combined.

3. Spoon the batter into the prepared muffin cups, dividing it evenly. Bake in the oven for 18–20 minutes, or until risen and firm to the touch. Cool in the pan for 5 minutes, then turn out onto a wire rack. Serve warm or cold.

NUTRITIONAL NOTE
Oat bran is a delicious source of soluble dietary fiber, which can help to reduce high blood cholesterol when eaten as part of a low fat diet.

HONEY & CINNAMON
Muffins

These muffins are relatively low in both fat and sugar. They're delicious served split and spread with a fruity conserve or concentrated fruit purée.

MAKES 10

1½ cups all-purpose flour
Generous ⅓ cup oatmeal, plus extra
   for sprinkling
¼ cup light brown sugar
2 teaspoons baking powder
½ teaspoon baking soda
¼ teaspoon salt
2 teaspoons ground cinnamon
1 egg, lightly beaten
⅔ cup skim milk
1 cup plain yogurt
¼ cup butter, melted
4 tablespoons clear honey

1. Preheat the oven to 400°F Grease 10 cups of a 12-cup muffin pan or line 10 cups with paper muffin cups.

2. Mix the flour, oatmeal, sugar, baking powder, baking soda, salt, and cinnamon in a large bowl. In a separate bowl, mix together the egg, milk, yogurt, melted butter, and honey. Add the wet ingredients all at once to the dry ingredients and mix briefly until just combined.

3. Spoon the batter into the prepared muffin cups, dividing it evenly, then sprinkle the tops with a little oatmeal. Bake in the oven for 18–20 minutes, or until well risen and golden. Cool in the pan for 5 minutes, then turn out onto a wire rack. Serve warm or cold.

NUTRITIONAL NOTE
Honey has a more intense sweetness than sugar, so you need less of it.

MUFFIN TIP
Fresh fruit such as raspberries, blackberries, or blueberries may be added to the mixture, if you like.

DATE BRAN Muffins

Make the batter for these muffins the day before you want to
bake them, as the batter needs to rest overnight.

MAKES 12

2 cups all-purpose flour
1 teaspoon baking soda
1 teaspoon ground cinnamon
1/2 cup superfine sugar
Generous 1 1/2 cups wheat bran
3/4 cup pitted dried or fresh dates,
   finely chopped
1/2 cup buttermilk
3/4 cup milk
3 tablespoons sunflower oil
1 egg, lightly beaten

1. Mix the flour, baking soda, cinnamon, and sugar in a large bowl. Add the wheat bran and dates and mix well.

2. In a separate small bowl, mix together the buttermilk, milk, sunflower oil, and egg. Add the egg mixture to the dry ingredients, mixing briefly until just combined. Cover and refrigerate overnight.

3. The next day, preheat the oven to 400°F. Grease a 12-cup muffin pan or line the cups with paper muffin cups.

4. Remove the batter from the fridge and spoon it into the prepared muffin cups, dividing it evenly. Bake in the oven for about 20 minutes, or until risen and golden. Cool in the pan for 10 minutes, then turn out onto a wire rack. Serve warm or cold.

GLUTEN-FREE PEANUT BUTTER, BANANA & CHOC-CHIP Muffins

MAKES 12

3 medium bananas

2 eggs, lightly beaten

$\frac{1}{2}$ cup light brown sugar

$\frac{1}{2}$ cup smooth peanut butter

Generous $\frac{1}{2}$ cup semi-sweet or milk chocolate chips

$1\frac{3}{4}$ cups white or brown rice flour

$1\frac{1}{2}$ teaspoons gluten-free baking powder

$\frac{1}{2}$ teaspoon baking soda

6 tablespoons butter, melted

$\frac{1}{2}$ cup buttermilk

1. Preheat the oven to 350°F. Grease a 12-cup muffin pan or line the cups with paper muffin cups.

2. Peel, then mash the bananas until fairly smooth in a large bowl, using a potato masher or fork. Stir in the eggs, sugar, and peanut butter until well mixed. Alternatively, put these ingredients in a blender or food processor and blend together until smooth.

3. Stir in the chocolate chips, then sift over the rice flour, baking powder and baking soda. In a separate bowl, mix together the melted butter and buttermilk. Pour the wet ingredients over the banana mixture and dry ingredients and mix briefly until just combined.

4. Spoon the batter into the prepared muffin cups, dividing it evenly. Bake in the oven for about 18–20 minutes, or until risen and golden. Cool in the pan for 10 minutes, then turn out onto a wire rack. Serve warm or cold.

MUFFIN TIP

Use really ripe bananas for these muffins as they add sweetness to the mixture and will mash more easily to a purée.

NUTRITIONAL NOTE

If you also need to avoid dairy products, substitute rice milk mixed with 1 teaspoon of lemon juice or white vinegar for buttermilk, use dairy-free fat spread instead of butter, and use dairy-free chocolate or carob chips.

APPLE, CHEESE & OAT Muffins

This unusual combination is positively delicious. Try serving these tasty and wholesome muffins for breakfast.

MAKES 12

1⅓ cups oat bran
½ cup whole-wheat flour
¼ cup light brown sugar
1½ tablespoons baking powder
1 teaspoon ground cinnamon
½ teaspoon salt
½ cup unsweetened apple juice
3 tablespoons skim milk
1 egg, lightly beaten
2 tablespoons sunflower oil
2 tablespoons clear honey
1 medium apple, peeled, cored, and diced
⅔ cup cheddar cheese, cut into small cubes
3 tablespoons rolled oats

1. Preheat the oven to 400°F. Grease a 12-cup muffin pan or line the cups with paper muffin cups.

2. Mix the oat bran, flour, sugar, baking powder, cinnamon, and salt in a large bowl. In a separate bowl, mix together the apple juice, milk, egg, sunflower oil, and honey. Add the wet ingredients to the dry ingredients, together with the diced apple and cheddar cheese, and mix briefly until just combined.

3. Spoon the batter into the prepared muffin cups, dividing it evenly, then sprinkle the tops with the oats. Bake in the oven for about 20 minutes, or until risen and golden. Cool in the pan for 10 minutes, then turn out onto a wire rack. Serve warm or cold.

GLUTEN-FREE APPLE, DATE & WALNUT Muffins

MUFFIN TIP
Unlike in other muffin recipes, the flours and other fine dry ingredients are sifted here to ensure that they are well-mixed and aerated.

MAKES **12**

1³/₄ cups white or brown rice flour

¹/₃ cup soy flour

2 teaspoons cornstarch

1 tablespoon gluten-free baking powder

¹/₂ teaspoon salt

1 teaspoon ground cinnamon

¹/₂ teaspoon ground pumpkin pie spice

Generous ¹/₂ cup unrefined superfine sugar

¹/₂ cup pitted dried dates, chopped

¹/₄ cup walnuts, chopped

2 eggs, lightly beaten

³/₄ cup milk

6 tablespoons sunflower oil

2 medium apples, peeled, cored, and finely chopped

FOR THE TOPPING

¹/₂ cup walnuts, chopped

2 tablespoons unrefined superfine sugar

1. Preheat the oven to 375°F. Grease a 12-cup muffin pan or line the cups with paper muffin cups.

2. For the muffins, sift the rice flour and soy flour, cornstarch, baking powder, salt, cinnamon, and pumpkin pie spice into a large bowl. Stir in the sugar, dates, and walnuts. In a separate bowl, mix together the eggs, milk, sunflower oil, and apples. Add this apple mixture all at once to the dry ingredients and mix briefly until just combined.

3. Spoon the batter into the prepared muffin cups, dividing it evenly. Mix together the topping ingredients in a small bowl, then sprinkle this mixture over the tops of the muffins.

4. Bake in the oven for about 20 minutes, or until risen and firm to the touch. Cool in the pan for 5 minutes, then turn out onto a wire rack. Serve warm or cold.

NUTRITIONAL NOTE
Gluten is a protein found in wheat and rye, and intolerance to this substance is a symptom of coeliac disease, an inflammatory condition of the gastrointestinal tract.

EGGLESS CHOCOLATE Muffins

These are such moist chocolatey muffins that no one will guess there's anything different about them.

MAKES 9

2 ounces creamed coconut (in a solid block), roughly chopped

6 tablespoons sunflower oil

1 1/2 cups self-rising flour

2 tablespoons unsweetened cocoa powder

1 teaspoon baking powder

Pinch of salt

1/2 cup light brown sugar

1. Preheat the oven to 350°F. Grease 9 cups of a 12-cup muffin pan or line 9 cups with paper muffin cups.

2. Pour 1 1/4 cups of boiling water into a bowl, add the creamed coconut and stir until it dissolves. Stir in the sunflower oil, then set aside to cool.

3. Mix the flour, cocoa powder, baking powder, salt, and brown sugar in a large bowl. Add the wet ingredients to the dry ingredients and stir briefly until just combined.

4. Spoon or ladle the batter into the prepared muffin cups, dividing it evenly. Bake in the oven for 15–18 minutes, or until well risen and firm to the touch. Cool in the pan for 5 minutes, then turn out onto a wire rack. Serve warm or cold.

NUTRITIONAL NOTE
These muffins are suitable for those who have a food intolerance or allergy to eggs and for vegans.

MUFFIN TIP
Use creamed coconut in a solid block rather than canned creamed coconut for these muffins.

HAZELNUT MINI Muffins

These mini savory muffins are delicious served with a simple soup.

MAKES 30

3 tablespoons peanut oil
²/₃ cup blanched hazelnuts, chopped
1 cup self-rising flour
½ cup self-rising whole-wheat flour
2 tablespoons cornmeal or instant polenta
½ teaspoon baking powder
Salt and freshly ground black pepper, to taste
1 egg, lightly beaten
¾ cup milk

NUTRITIONAL NOTE
Hazelnuts are a rich source of vitamin E. As well as being a powerful antioxidant, this vitamin helps to keep the heart healthy by preventing the oxidation of LDL cholesterol.

1. Preheat the oven to 375°F. Grease two 12-cup non-stick mini muffin pans and one 6-cup non-stick mini muffin pan, or one 24-cup non-stick mini muffin pan and one 6-cup non-stick mini muffin pan.

2. Heat 1 tablespoon of the peanut oil in a non-stick skillet. Add half of the chopped hazelnuts and cook over a low heat for a few minutes until the nuts are just beginning to color. Remove the pan from the heat and stir in the rest of the peanut oil to stop the nuts from cooking further. Set aside.

3. Mix the flours, cornmeal or polenta, baking powder, and salt and pepper in a large bowl. In a separate bowl, mix together the egg and milk. Stir in the toasted hazelnuts and oil mixture. Add the wet ingredients to the dry ingredients and mix briefly until just combined.

4. Spoon the batter into the prepared muffin cups, dividing it evenly, then sprinkle the tops with the remaining hazelnuts, pressing them gently into the batter. Bake in the oven for 10–12 minutes, or until well risen and golden brown. Cool in the pans for 5 minutes, then turn out onto a wire rack. Serve warm or cold.

WHOLE-WHEAT BANANA & WALNUT Muffins

The whole-wheat flour in this recipe really brings out the nutty flavor in these delicious muffins.

MAKES 12

1 cup self-rising whole-wheat flour
1 cup self-rising flour
2 tablespoons light brown sugar
1/2 cup walnuts, chopped
3 large very ripe bananas, peeled
3 tablespoons sunflower oil
2 eggs, lightly beaten
5 tablespoons sour cream
2 tablespoons clear honey

1. Preheat the oven to 400°F. Grease a 12-cup muffin pan or line the cups with paper muffin cups.

2. Mix the flours, sugar, and walnuts in a large bowl. In a separate bowl, mash the bananas until fairly smooth using a potato masher or fork, then stir in the sunflower oil, eggs, sour cream, and honey.

3. Add the wet ingredients all at once to the dry ingredients and mix briefly until just combined. Spoon the batter into the prepared muffin cups, dividing it evenly.

4. Bake in the oven for about 20 minutes, or until risen and golden. Cool in the pan for 10 minutes, then turn out onto a wire rack. Serve warm or cold.

COTTAGE CHEESE & RAISIN Muffins

This unusual combination of savory and sweet works really well and creates very moist muffins.

MAKES 12

2 cups all-purpose flour
1 1/2 cups toasted bran sticks, such as
    All-Bran cereal
3/4 cup superfine sugar
1 tablespoon baking powder
1/2 teaspoon baking soda
1 teaspoon ground cinnamon
1 teaspoon finely grated orange zest
1/2 teaspoon salt
Generous 1 cup cottage cheese
1 cup plain yogurt
2 tablespoons clear honey
1/4 cup butter, melted
2 eggs, lightly beaten
1/2 cup peeled carrots, grated
1/2 cup raisins
FOR THE TOPPING
2 tablespoons sugar
1 teaspoon ground cinnamon

1. Preheat the oven to 400°F. Grease a 12-cup muffin pan or line the cups with paper muffin cups.

2. Mix the flour, toasted bran cereal, sugar, baking powder, baking soda, cinnamon, orange zest, and salt in a large bowl.

3. In a separate bowl, mix together the cottage cheese, yogurt, honey, melted butter, and eggs. Add the wet ingredients to the dry ingredients and mix briefly until just combined. Fold in the carrots and raisins.

4. Spoon the batter into the prepared muffin cups, dividing it evenly. Combine the sugar and cinnamon for the topping, then sprinkle this mixture over the tops of the muffins. Bake in the oven for 20–25 minutes, or until risen and golden. Cool in the pan for 10 minutes, then turn out onto a wire rack. Serve warm or cold.

GLUTEN-FREE FRESH BLUEBERRY Muffins

Suitable for a gluten-free diet, these simple fruit muffins

will soon become a perennial favorite.

MAKES 9

½ cup rice flour

½ cup soy or potato flour

½ cup superfine sugar

¼ teaspoon salt

2 teaspoons gluten-free baking powder

2 eggs, lightly beaten

½ cup milk

2 tablespoons lemon juice

1 cup fresh blueberries

1. Preheat the oven to 350°F. Grease 9 cups of a 12-cup muffin pan or line 9 cups with paper muffin cups.

2. Mix the flours, sugar, salt, and baking powder in a large bowl. In a separate bowl, mix together the eggs, milk, and lemon juice. Add the wet ingredients all at once to the dry ingredients, tip in the blueberries, and mix briefly until just combined.

3. Spoon the batter into the prepared muffin cups, dividing it evenly. Bake in the oven for about 20 minutes, or until risen and golden. Cool in the pan for 5 minutes, then turn out onto a wire rack. Serve warm or cold.

NUTRITIONAL NOTE
Blueberries are a good source of vitamin C and beta-carotene, both powerful antioxidants.

MUFFIN TIP
Rice and soy flours have a heavier texture than wheat flour, but the acid from the lemon juice reacts with the baking powder to give these muffins a better rise.

OAT & CHERRY Muffins

These whole-wheat muffins are given a slightly nutty texture with the addition of rolled oats. They're delicious for a mid-morning snack and will keep up energy levels until lunchtime.

MAKES 10

½ cup rolled oats
Scant 1¼ cups milk
2 teaspoons vanilla extract
1½ cups self-rising whole-wheat flour
1 teaspoon baking powder
½ teaspoon salt
¾ cup light brown sugar
½ cup dried sweetened cherries, chopped
1 egg, lightly beaten
6 tablespoons sunflower oil
Generous ¼ cup powdered sugar (preferably unrefined), sifted

1. Preheat the oven to 375°F. Grease 10 cups of a 12-cup muffin pan or line 10 cups with paper muffin cups.

2. Put the oats in a medium bowl and pour over the milk and vanilla extract. Stir briefly, then set aside to soak for 10 minutes.

3. Mix the flour, baking powder, salt, and brown sugar in a large bowl. Add half the chopped cherries to the flour mixture. Stir the egg and sunflower oil into the oat mixture. Add the oat mixture to the dry ingredients and mix briefly until just combined.

4. Spoon the batter into the prepared muffin cups, dividing it evenly. Bake in the oven for about 20 minutes, or until well risen and firm to the touch. Cool in the pan for 5 minutes, then turn out onto a wire rack and leave to cool completely.

5. Blend the powdered sugar with 2 teaspoons of warm water in a small bowl to make an almost transparent, thin, smooth icing. Stir in the remaining dried cherries. Spoon some of this icing on top of each muffin. Leave until the icing has set before serving.

NUTRITIONAL NOTE
Rolled oats are whole oat grains that have been husked and then rolled to flatten, so they contain all the nutrients of the whole grain.

MUFFIN TIP
The icing adds a decorative touch to these muffins, but you can serve them simply dusted with a little powdered sugar (preferably unrefined), if you prefer.

HONEY OAT BRAN Muffins

These lightly spiced oat bran muffins create a tasty snack, ideal for breakfast on the go or to pop into lunchboxes.

MAKES 12

1¼ cups self-rising flour

1 cup self-rising whole-wheat flour

½ teaspoon ground pumpkin pie spice

5 tablespoons light brown sugar

1 tablespoon baking powder

⅓ cup oat bran

⅔ cup golden raisins

6 tablespoons sunflower oil

3 tablespoons clear honey, plus about 3 tablespoons to drizzle

2 eggs, lightly beaten

1 cup milk

1. Preheat the oven to 400°F. Grease a 12-cup muffin pan or line the cups with paper muffin cups.

2. Mix the flours, pumpkin pie spice, sugar, baking powder, and oat bran in a large bowl. Add the golden raisins and mix well.

3. In a separate bowl, mix together the sunflower oil, 3 tablespoons honey, the eggs, and milk. Add the egg mixture to the dry ingredients and mix briefly until just combined.

4. Spoon the batter into the prepared muffin cups, dividing it evenly. Bake in the oven for 20–25 minutes, or until risen and golden. Drizzle about 1 teaspoon of honey over the top of each hot baked muffin. Cool in the pan for 10 minutes, then turn out onto a wire rack. Serve warm or cold.

MUFFIN TIP

Oat bran should be available in supermarkets near the rolled oats, but if you have any difficulty in finding it, try your local health food store.

HIGH-FIBER Muffins

Although these muffins are fairly low in fat and sugar, juices from the carrot and banana will ensure they stay beautifully moist and will help to sweeten them as well.

MAKES 12

1 cup self-rising flour
¾ cup self-rising whole-wheat flour
2 teaspoons baking powder
½ teaspoon ground cinnamon
½ teaspoon ground ginger
¼ cup light brown sugar
Pinch of salt
1 large ripe banana, peeled and
    roughly chopped
1 large carrot, coarsely grated
½ cup golden raisins
⅓ cup hazelnuts, chopped
1 egg, lightly beaten
¼ cup sunflower margarine, melted
1 cup skimmed milk

1. Preheat the oven to 400°F. Grease a 12-cup muffin pan or line the cups with paper muffin cups.

2. Mix the flours, baking powder, cinnamon, ginger, sugar and salt in a large bowl. Stir in the banana, carrot, golden raisins and hazelnuts. In a separate bowl, mix together the egg, melted margarine, and milk. Add the wet ingredients to the dry ingredients and mix until just combined.

3. Spoon the batter into the prepared muffin cups, dividing it evenly. Bake in the oven for about 20 minutes, or until well risen and firm to the touch. Cool in the pan for 10 minutes, then turn out onto a wire rack. Serve warm or cold.

NUTRITIONAL NOTE
Using sunflower margarine instead of butter adds flavor to the muffins and ensures that they are low in saturated fat too.

MUFFIN TIP
While most muffins should be eaten within a day of making (or frozen as soon as they are cool), moist muffins like these can be kept for up to three days in an airtight container in the fridge.

INDEX

RECIPE CREDITS

CATHERINE ATKINSON: PAGES 28, 29, 30, 33, 34, 38, 40, 42, 46, 48, 50, 51, 60, 61, 62, 68, 70, 72, 74, 80, 81, 82, 90, 94, 97, 98, 99, 101, 102, 104, 105, 106, 110, 116, 118, 122, 126, 129, 130, 131, 132, 136, 142, 144, 145, 148, 154, 156, 162, 169, 170, 172, 175, 176, 178, 181, 182, 185

CAROL TENNANT: PAGES 26, 32, 36, 37, 41, 44, 45, 47, 52, 53, 54, 58, 64, 65, 66, 67, 71, 75, 76, 78, 79, 84, 85, 86, 87, 88, 91, 92, 93, 96, 100, 112, 113, 114, 115, 119, 120, 121, 124, 125, 128, 134, 135, 140, 141, 146, 147, 150, 151, 152, 153, 157, 158, 160, 161, 166, 168, 171, 174, 179, 180, 184